FARM STREET

FARM STREET

THE STORY OF THE JESUITS' CHURCH IN LONDON

MICHAEL HALL, SHERIDAN GILLEY AND MARIA PERRY

WITH SPECIAL PHOTOGRAPHY
BY ANDREW TWORT

[signatures]

Peter Sanbudge

Ciaq
x x x x x
x x x

First published in 2016 by Unicorn,
an imprint of Unicorn Publishing Group LLP
101 Wardour Street
London W1F 0UG
www.unicornpublishing.org

ISBN 978-1-910787-64-9

10 9 8 7 6 5 4 3 2 1

Produced by Tiggy Butler Publishing Ltd
Editorial direction: Peter Sawbridge
  (Long Meadow Press Ltd)
Consultant: Dr Thierry Morel
Picture researcher: Sara Ayad
Designer: Maggi Smith
Indexer: Hilary Bird
Colour origination: Gomer Press Ltd

Printed in Wales by Gomer Press Ltd

EDITORIAL NOTE
At the Church of the Immaculate Conception,
liturgical east in fact faces north. Throughout
this book, the geographical rather than the
liturgical points of the compass are used in
descriptions of the building.

The discursive captions accompanying
Andrew Twort's newly commissioned
photographs are the work of Michael Hall.

Except where otherwise stated, all
documents and portrait photographs
reproduced come from the Archives of
the Jesuits in Britain.

ILLUSTRATIONS
Page 2: a detail of the north window, depicting
the Tree of Jesse, made by Hardman of
Birmingham and installed in 1912, replacing
the original glass by William Wailes.

Pages 4–5: the vault over the Calvary Chapel,
designed by W. H. Romaine-Walker. The
idea of piercing the vault with tracery may
have been derived from the Chapel of the
Constable of Castile at Burgos Cathedral.

Pages 6–7: the west aisle, designed by W. H.
Romaine-Walker and completed in 1903.
The chapels alternate with confessionals,
below the windows. On the right is the Chapel
of St Thomas the Apostle. Its altarpiece, by
Julia Gambardella, is adapted from a painting
of around 1505 by Cima da Conegliano in the
Gallerie dell'Accademia, Venice. The statue
of St Thomas of Canterbury, far right, is by
Charles Whiffen. The saint's crozier is made
of ivory and ormolu.

ACKNOWLEDGEMENTS
My deepest gratitude goes to Peter
Sawbridge, Editorial Director at the Royal
Academy of Arts. Introduced to the project
by our mutual friend, the acclaimed
exhibition curator Thierry Morel, Peter has
breathed happy life into every element
of this book, bringing together those
who excel in their own fields. Sheridan
Gilley and Michael Hall, to whom I owe
my most respectful thanks, have given
us authoritative accounts of the church's
foundation and earlier history and of
its sublime architecture and decoration.
Rebecca Somerset and Mary Allen have
answered numerous research enquiries in
the Archives of the Jesuits in Britain at Farm
Street, Sara Ayad has undertaken the picture
research with great skill and tenacity, and
Maggi Smith has designed this sumptuous
layout for us. All have given of their talent
to create a book in which word and image
are seamlessly combined. I owe a special
debt of gratitude to Andrew Twort, whose
remarkable photographs are enjoyed around
the world. Beauty is an extraordinary gift,
and Andrew's lens fills pages of this book
with it: I hope his images will captivate our
readers and draw them to Farm Street to
discover it for themselves. Last, but in no
way least, my gratitude goes to Fr Andrew
Cameron-Mowat SJ, who has graciously
permitted me to produce this book, and
whose introduction to the historian
and author Maria Perry has given us an
enchanting and memorable account of
Farm Street's more recent history and
the church's contemporary life.

Tiggy Butler

CONTENTS

THE HISTORY OF FARM STREET TO 1914
SHERIDAN GILLEY
11

THE ARCHITECTURE AND FURNISHINGS
OF THE CHURCH AND THE ASSOCIATED BUILDINGS
IN FARM STREET AND MOUNT STREET
MICHAEL HALL
31

FARM STREET BETWEEN THE WARS
AND BEYOND
MARIA PERRY
93

ENDNOTES
114

FURTHER READING
PHOTOGRAPHIC ACKNOWLEDGEMENTS
117

INDEX
118

SHERIDAN GILLEY

THE HISTORY OF FARM STREET TO 1914

Farm Street had humble beginnings.[1] The Catholic Relief Act of 1829 still envisioned the suppression of the Society of Jesus and of other religious orders, and there were then only 109 English Jesuits: 54 priests, 47 scholastics and eight brothers. The Jesuit presence in London in 1824 was a small day school for boys in Norton Street, which moved in 1830 to the Marylebone Road. It closed in 1836. Its most distinguished pupil was the gifted illustrator

and antiquary James Doyle,[2] uncle to Sir Arthur Conan Doyle and brother of the cartoonist Richard ('Dick Kitcat') Doyle,[3] who was to resign from *Punch* over its attacks upon the restoration of the Roman Catholic hierarchy of diocesan bishops in 1850.[4] In 1833 Fr Edward Scott[5] was followed as Superior of the London house by the remarkably active and energetic Fr Randall Lythgoe (fig. 2),[6] who became Provincial in 1841, and was all but the refounder of the Society of Jesus in Britain, through churches, missions and schools. Perhaps Lythgoe's most influential single action was to receive the young Quaker Frederick Lucas into the Church in December 1838, and then to put him forward a little more than a year later as the founding editor of the weekly newspaper *The Tablet*. Lucas was a champion of the Irish poor and of the Society of Jesus, and *The Tablet* became the most influential and unpacifically Quaker journalistic organ of Victorian Roman Catholicism.[7]

The establishment of *The Tablet* was itself significant of a new confidence in the Roman Catholic Church in England. In 1839 the Jesuit Provincial at Worcester, Fr John Bird,[8] received £700 from an 'Unknown' correspondent, with a covering note (fig. 3), franked Blackburn, 3 November, which displayed an equal confidence:

> *AMDG To a subscription towards building a Church in London to be dedicated to the Ever Immaculate Blessed Virgin and to be called 'The Immaculate Conception'.*
>
> *Offer up with heart & soul every Saturday the Holy Sacrifice of the Mass in honor of the Immaculate Conception for the reconversion of England & if this devotion become general we may be certain of the reestablishment of the true faith in our unhappy country.*[9]

Fig. 1
A view south through the inner aisle of the double west aisle. Its architect, W. H. Romaine-Walker, drew inspiration from the Decorated style of mid-fourteenth-century England, notably the Lady Chapel at Ely Cathedral. At the far end is a Della Robbia sculpture of the Madonna and Child (see fig. 75).

Fig. 2
Fr Randall Lythgoe, before 1842.
Photographer unknown

A M D G

in London

To a subscription towards building a Church, to be dedicated to the Ever Immaculate Blessed Virgin and to be called "The Immaculate Conception."

ARCH. PROV. ANG. S. J. OCTOBER, 1960

Offer up with heart & soul every saturday the Holy Sacrifice of the Mass in honour of the Immaculate Conception for the reconversion of England & if this devotion become general we may be certain of the reestablisment of the true faith in our unhappy Country

Blackburn is only eleven miles from the Jesuit college of Stonyhurst, and the secret donor, whose name has been well kept, must have been known to some. On 28 December, Fr Thomas Glover,[10] the Jesuit agent in Rome, wrote to Lythgoe: 'I must now tell you, on the part of the [Jesuit] General, that no time is to be lost in making a beginning of a church and house in London.'[11]

The dedication was testament to the rising tide of nineteenth-century Marian devotion, supremely enshrined in the definition of the dogma of the Immaculate Conception as binding on Roman Catholics by Pope Pius IX in 1854, and confirmed by the apparition to St Bernadette Soubirous at Lourdes in 1858. The church's first Rector, from 1841 until 1854,[12] was Fr James Brownbill (fig. 4), who was 'never regarded as bright', according to one Jesuit historian, 'with no pretensions and no taste', 'a simple, average, unaffected man of no great intellectual attainments'.[13] The building was designed as 'a preacher's church with no screen and a short sanctuary, but equipped with a fine altar erection by Pugin'.[14] The early emphasis on preaching is significant of the many orators who were to occupy the community's pulpit. The clergy house between 1845 and 1849 was at 25 Bolton Street, Piccadilly.[15] Though resident at various addresses in the area, including 9 Hill Street from 1846 and 111 Mount Street in 1868, and briefly at 31 Farm Street in 1886, the community was only to find its permanent home in the present buildings at 114 Mount Street in December 1887.

In planning for a church in the capital, the Society's aspirations were national rather than parochial: to provide a metropolitan centre for its own lay following 'in the most eligible part of London', as Lythgoe put it, announcing the acquisition of the site to Glover in Rome in 1841.[16] The subscription lists for the new church show their clientele to have included parts of the Catholic aristocracy, gentry and well-to-do lay alumni of their schools. Subscribers included Sir Charles Tempest,[17] who gave £500, his wife £500, and his daughter Monica another £50 – she later contributed £1,500 for Pugin's high altar – while the medieval Romantic writer K. H. Digby,[18] Lords Petre[19] and Stourton[20] and Henry Maxwell[21] all gave £100. The subscribers' list included the Hon. Charles Langdale,[22] of Houghton Hall, near Market Weighton in the East Riding, a former MP, the son of a former Lord Stourton and the doyen of London Catholic charitable and educational institutions as 'the acknowledged father and patriarch of the oppressed Catholic community in England'.[23] He was to take 'vows of devotion' on his deathbed as a lay brother of the Society. He gave £50.[24] Fifty scudi came from Cardinal James Fransoni, another fifty from the English Curial Cardinal Charles Acton (fig. 5),[25] son of a Shropshire baronet who had been Prime Minister of Naples, and two hundred from the English colony in Rome, pleading against a large north window 'lest devotion be killed by too much light'.[26] In total, these donations amounted to a large sum, but then the leasehold on the land for the church was worth £5,856. The freehold

CHARLES CARDINAL ACTON BORN 6 MARCH 1803, OB: 27 JUNE 1847 BURIED AT NAPLES.

Fig. 5
Vincenzo Morani,
Cardinal Charles Acton, 1844.
Oil on canvas, 75 × 62 cm.
National Trust, Coughton Court,
991136

of the church was only bought for £23,000 from the Berkeley Estate in March 1891.[27] £5,843.12.4 had been given by 1846, rising to £9,249.6.8 by 1850.[28] 'Friends in Flanders gave a monstrance, nuns in Lyons sent altar linen and one Continental benefactor thoughtfully provided a green baize bag lest a chasuble, in silver lamé, should be damaged by the London fogs.'[29]

The difficulties with erecting the new church were not with money but with ecclesiastical authority, and were part of the long-term conflict between the secular and regular clergy in the Roman Catholic Church in England. The Vicar Apostolic of the London District, Bishop James Bramston,[30] had prevented the Jesuits from acquiring a church at St John's Wood in the 1830s, built by two sisters called Gallini, and on 16 June 1841 his successor Thomas Griffiths,[31] in Jesuit opinion 'a man of cool conduct, inflexible[,] a known enemy to regulars',[32] refused permission for the new church on the grounds that it was too close to the old Bavarian Embassy Chapel in Warwick Street and would take away that parish's income for baptisms, weddings and funerals. Griffiths added that he himself intended 'to erect a Cathedral at this end of the Town, in place of one of the present Chapels'. With the compelling argument that his diocese was overwhelmed with pauper immigrants from Ireland, he offered the Society four places for a chapel in London where they might evangelise these poor: 'where Cambridge road crosses the Regents Canal; between that spot, & Mile End Road; Saffron Hill; & Brixton ... where hundreds would be sanctified by the near residence of zealous Pastors.'[33]

By no means averse to such evangelisation, the Jesuits used the argument that their church was needed because the number of Catholic baptisms in London suggested that there were more Catholics in the British capital than in Rome. They also insisted that their site was at a canonical distance from other chapels, and near the former Portuguese Embassy Chapel in South Audley Street, Grosvenor Square, in fact just around the corner, which because of civil war in Portugal had closed in 1829, when it had three chaplains (down from six in 1805). The Jesuits thought that the Vicar Apostolic and his clergy were 'studiously impressing on the minds of the People that our object is not to do good, but to gain influence amongst the rich':[34] why else should the Society refuse a mission to a poorer area such as the crowded tenements of Saffron Hill?

The Society had the support of Cardinal Acton, as the matter went to the Congregation of Propaganda Fide, which was responsible for England as a missionary territory, and which in a Rescript of 23 April 1843 (fig. 6)[35] granted permission for the erection of the church in London. However, it met the Bishop's objections judicially, by denying Farm Street the ordinary parochial status to perform baptisms, marriages and funerals, and exacting from it a £30 annual payment towards a poor mission, with another £30 to the Vicar Apostolic. The condition of the provision of a poor mission was directly fulfilled when the Jesuits took charge in 1850 of St Mary's, Horseferry Road, in Westminster (they relinquished it after half a century in 1901). The number of priests at Farm Street was not to exceed those of the former Portuguese Embassy Chapel. The Jesuits were still indignant at the 'hard and shameful'[36] conditions being imposed on them, even while accepting them, arguing that the money provision was in defiance of the oath of allegiance,[37] and on 7 May 1844 a petition appealing against the decision with more than seventy signatures, including those of Lords Stourton and Petre, was presented to the Pope by Sir William Lawson,[38] who had just been made a Knight of the Order of Christ to add to his new English baronetcy. The petition was received politely but without effect.[39] As Lythgoe himself acknowledged, it was worth 'great sacrifices' that a 'great object' had been secured.[40] It should be said here that for all their high-born following, the Jesuits laid a particular emphasis in their teaching and preaching on generosity to the poor, of which more is said below.

At the laying of the foundation stone, on the Feast of St Ignatius, 31 July 1844, *The Tablet* remarked that 'attendance, if not very numerous, was certainly *distingué*, including a very large proportion of ladies'. The lay mason on the occasion was the Hon. Edward Petre, like Langdale a former MP and a prominent and tireless figure in London Catholic charitable activity, who after a financial crisis had devoted himself to good works: he had given up racing after his horses Matilda, The Colonel and Rowton had won the St Leger Stakes three years running.[41] 'A large wooden cross was therefore sunk in the earth at the northern extremity of the ground, on the spot where the high altar will hereafter rise, with the foundation stone near it to the north-west', inscribed with 'July 31st, Ao. Xi. (Anno Christi, in the Year of Christ), 1844'. However, 'to the surprise of most who were present, the Rev. Mr Lythgoe took occasion to observe that a report had been assiduously, perhaps studiously, spread abroad that ample funds were at command for the completion of the intended structure', but that 'he could solemnly and truly assure them that there were no funds whatever in existence applicable to that object...' This may have been misreported – certainly a proportion of the cost had been raised – as Lythgoe's audience included existing subscribers. The reporter remarked that the occasion required the approval of a bishop, but Griffiths was away. 'In the absence of the venerable diocesan, the

ad honestiorem antistitis sustentationem curandam, Patres Societatis
Jesu per singulos annos ad Triginta Sterlinas libras Vicario Apostolico
Londinensi pro tempore existenti titulo Cathedratici oblationis exsolven-
das obstringentur.

    Datum Romae ex Aedibus dictae Sacrae Congregationis de Pro-
paganda Fide Die, et anno quibus supra —

    Gratis sine ulla omnin... ...quocumque titulo

...nes Brunelli S. Congnis de Pr...
Fide Secrius

N. Pedini

N. Rosker

Ex Audientia Sanctissimi. Die 13. Aprilis 1843.

    Cum Emis Patribus Sacrae Congregationis de Propaganda Fide in
Conventu habito die 23. Januarii dignum fuerit stabiliendam esse ydonio-
rem concordiam inter Vicarium Apostolicum Londinensem, et Patres Societatis Jesu in his, quae pertinent ad novam Ecclesiam per ipsos Patres in Urbe
Londini erigendam; Sanctissimus Dominus Noster Gregorius Divina Provi-
dentia Papa XVI., rationibus quae ex utraque parte allatae sunt, beni-
gne auditis, omnibusque mature perpensis ac serio consideratis, consilium
a nonnullis Emis Cardinalibus ad hoc a Sacra Congregatione delectis
propositum pro singulari sua indulgentia adprobavit. Ut itaque Divi-
no Cultui promovendo, et Catholicae Religioni non minus conservandae
quam amplificandae magis magisque consuleretur, auctoritate Sanctissimi sancitum est ut sequitur. I. Integrum erit Patribus Societatis
Jesu in Urbe Londini, ac praecise secus Viam Farm-Street in Districtu
Warwick Domum sibi atque Ecclesiam extruere super aream ipsis
in hunc finem attributam. 2. Minime tamen fas erit memoratis
Patribus in Eadem Ecclesia Sacramentum Baptismatis administrare,
aut matrimoniis adsistere, aut demum cadavera sepelire: quum haec
sint pura exclusive parochialia, a quibus Patres Societatis Jesu prae-
sentis Decreti tenore omnino prohibentur, ...que proinde penes
aliam Ecclesiam non longe ab noviter erigenda jamdiu existentem,
et ad Legationem Bavarici Regni spectantem sarta tecta mane-
bunt. 3. Erit insuper ipsorum Patrum aliquem e sua Societate
Evangelicum Operarium ad aliam praedictae Urbis regionem, ubi
populus spiritualibus auxiliis magis indigeat, ab Vicario Apostolico Londinensi designandam, statis ab eo diebus mittere, ut in illa
nimirum Sacramenta fidelibus administret, donec saltem media sup-
petant ad Ecclesiam inibi etiam aedificandam, cujus servitio ejus-
dem Societatis Patres, conditionibus tunc, ut par erit praescribendis,
mancipentur. 4. Ecclesia Legationis Bavaricae, mox ut parata
fuerit altera per Societatis Jesu Patres, quemadmodum supra dictum
est, extruenda, ab obligatione pendendi quotannis Ecclesiae in Loco
Westminster erectae Summam Triginta Librarum Sterlinarum prorsus
eximetur; quae quidem obligatio deinde in Ecclesiam dictam prae-
nunciatae Societatis transibit ab iisque implenda erit. 5. Ostre-
...mo in argumentum obsequii erga Episcopalem auctoritatem, atque...

...aprile 1843. ...Monsignor
...ente si fa anche un dover...
...Santità istessa, che nella...
...bia ad osservi un numer...
...che vi era nell'antica ...

A sua
N. Rosker

ceremonial was, of course, divested of all its pontifical pomp, but the solemn impressiveness of the occasion … could not fail to awe…'[42]

The building of the church was supposed to take eighteen months, but it was not opened until exactly five years later, on the Feast of St Ignatius, 31 July 1849. By then, the appointment of Nicholas Wiseman as Pro-Vicar Apostolic of the London District in 1847 (and Vicar Apostolic in February 1849) represented a revolution in episcopal attitudes to the Society. Wiseman had high hopes of the regulars, and preached at the opening on the glories of the Jesuit Order, as the practitioners of their founder's *Spiritual Exercises*, as champions of the Counter-Reformation, as writers, scholars and teachers, and as foreign missionaries and organisers of charity. Wiseman was attended by William Wareing, Vicar Apostolic of the Eastern District,[43] by Bishop Brown of Wales,[44] who preached at the evening service, by Bishop Gillis,[45] assistant to the Vicar Apostolic of the Scottish Eastern District, and by a hundred priests. Admission was by ticket, costing a sovereign. The collection fetched £100. The preachers on the Sunday following were two trophy Oxford converts from Anglicanism: Frederick Oakeley,[46] formerly chaplain and Fellow of Balliol, and John Henry Newman's disciple, the Oratorian Frederick William Faber,[47] who had just (on 31 May) opened the Oratory in London.[48] The Redemptorists had also recently (in 1848) set up their house in Clapham, as the work of the religious orders was encouraged by Wiseman himself.

In fact, in 1852 Wiseman expressed to Fr Faber his discontent with what the orders in general and the Jesuits in particular were then doing as missionary work among the poor; and certainly Farm Street itself was not a poor man's church.[49] The schedule completed by Fr Brownbill for the Religious Census on Sunday 31 March 1851 (fig. 7), a unique exercise on a national scale, indicates that only one hundred of its five hundred sittings were free.[50] The church was, however, well attended, with about four hundred worshippers at the High Mass, between fifty and a hundred at each of the three other Masses, and around two hundred at the afternoon service – and this at a time of year outside the main months of the season, when many members of its larger congregations would not have been in London.

There were two later, local attempts at a religious census in London, organised by Liberal Nonconformist newspapers. The first, conducted by the *British Weekly* on a single day in 1886, unfortunately 'took no account of any services, either Masses of the Roman Catholic Church or early Communions of the Established Church, preceding the 11 a.m. service',[51] and is therefore useless as a count of those who fulfilled their Catholic obligation. In the *Daily News* census, held between November 1902 and November 1903, in a city with many more Catholic churches than in 1851, the Farm Street congregations on one Sunday numbered 303 men, 617 women and 128 children at morning Mass, a total of 1,048; and a total of 493 – 144 men, 290 women and 59 children – at its later services.[52] These last, of course, were not Masses and therefore not of

A RETURN

OF THE SEVERAL PARTICULARS TO BE INQUIRED INTO RESPECTING THE UNDERMENTIONED

PLACE OF PUBLIC RELIGIOUS WORSHIP.

obligation, and could be assumed to have attracted those who had been to Mass already. This predominance of women over men was a general feature of Anglican and Catholic congregations in England, and the ratio of two to one was not unusual.

How Farm Street was seen by strangers is summed up by Charles Booth in his seven-volume Edwardian series *Religious Influences*, the third section of his *Life and Labour of the People in London*.[53] Booth's principal interest in this series lay in the social influence of religious institutions and in the alienation of so many of the English poor from organised religion.[54] He also eschewed the numerical methods of the attempts at a census, although his coloured map of the neighbourhood of the church showed it to be overwhelmingly in his richest 'Wealthy' category, marked in yellow.[55] The neighbourhood had been a mixed one, but in the last two decades of the nineteenth century the Grosvenor Estate proceeded to eliminate its last corners of poverty. Indeed in some ways Farm Street resembled the proprietary chapels for the well-to-do that abounded in the neighbourhood, such as the nearby Grosvenor Chapel:

> *The Chapel of the Jesuits, in Farm Street, is allotted no particular district and does not need one. It is a church for the rich, and especially for propaganda amongst the rich. The services are numerous and attractive, the singing good, the ceremonial perfect; the building surprisingly beautiful, and the preachers gifted men. There is no service in the evening, 'their people dine late'. The work extends into other fields: fields of literature and controversy. The presbytery will accommodate a considerably larger number than those who are in more permanent residence, and is used almost like a hotel by many others of the Order who come and go through London.*[56]

The large quantity of Jesuit visitors from elsewhere, then as now, is an important point. Booth was himself struck with the seriousness of devotion of observant Catholics.

Booth's entry is based on an interview of 17 February 1899 with Fr Alexander Charnley[57] (Rector 1898–1904; fig. 8), who impressed the unknown interviewer: 'Personally, he is an interesting man, clever, courteous, smiling, confident.' Also impressive was Fr Joseph Bampton[58] (Rector 1894–98; fig. 9), who began a series of four sermons on the Pope on 19 February with a congregation of around four hundred. The dominant note struck by the interviewer is one of admiration if not agreement. The church building was said to hold six to seven hundred, with around six hundred at the Sunday High Mass, and the clergy to make around a hundred converts a year, 'a considerable portion' of them being well educated. Having no parish, and

Fig. 10
Fr William Waterworth.
Photograph F. C. Hahl, Worcester

Fig. 11
Fr Henry Mahon.
Photograph A. S. Watson, Great Yarmouth

Fig. 12
Fr William Cobb.
Photograph W. Dreeser, Liverpool

not wanting one, the Jesuits 'have to tempt people to them, and all the world knows how successfully they do this'. The interviewer remarks that 'Farm St with the Oratory, and to a lesser extent, the pro-Cathedral at Kensington are the fashionable Roman Catholic Churches in London ... It doubtless focuses much of the intellectual energy of Catholicism':

> *Money appears to be plentiful; the house itself is chargeable with £300 a year in rates and taxes alone, £500 a year is said to be spent in charitable relief. They [the Jesuits] appear to have given up the attempt to work with the C.O.S.[59] or to do the work on a careful basis, except in the exercise of the best private judgement. People come to them from many private parts, and the majority are not the very destitute, but those needing something more than a meal. Father C. admits that they are taken in at times, but thinks that this cannot be helped.[60]*

This piecemeal need was certainly a marked contrast with the nearby parish of Our Lady of the Rosary, with its huge shifting population of the destitute Irish poor.[61]

Again, from its earliest days the church and its community achieved a continuity and security in the stability of its patterns of religious observance and its liturgical and devotional life. The resident priests in 1856 were Fathers William Waterworth (Rector 1854–57; fig. 10),[62] Henry Mahon (fig. 11),[63] Henry Segrave[64] and Edward T. Hood.[65] The Sunday and Holy Day Masses were at 7.30 am, 8.30 am and 9.30 am, with High Mass at 11 am. The weekday Masses were at 7.30 am, 8.30 am and 10 am. Vespers on Sundays and Holy Days were at 3.30 pm, with Instruction and Benediction. On the first Sunday of the month, the Devotion of the Bona Mors took place at 3.30 pm instead of Vespers. On Wednesday evenings there were Stations of the Cross and Benediction at 8 pm.

Fr Waterworth established the Confraternity of the Bona Mors, of the Sacred Heart of Jesus and of the Immaculate Heart of Mary,[66] whose members were listed in a letter from Fr William Cobb (fig. 12)[67] to Wiseman in 1849, together with proposed devotions to the Jesuit Saints Ignatius, Xavier and Aloysius.[68] The Bona Mors Confraternity, founded in 1852, was a hardy perennial: a census of membership of 1902–03 lists more than two thousand names.[69] The listing might have been suggested by an exercise that failed, the contemporary Archconfraternity of Our Lady of Compassion 'for the return of Great Britain to the Catholic Faith', established in 1897.[70] Farm Street was the first church to set up the Archconfraternity, which attracted more than fifteen hundred members, but it quickly passed away. The prayers used by the early Confraternities are set out in a small book, *Prayers and Devotional Exercises Used at the Church of the Immaculate Conception, Farm Street, Berkeley Square*.[71] By 1862, there was a Sunday service of Devotion to the Sacred Heart with Sermon and Benediction at 4 pm. There were now nine

resident clergy,[72] and eight in 1873,[73] one of them the Provincial, Fr Robert Whitty (fig. 13),[74] an Irishman who had tried his vocation as an Oratorian and was another of Newman's friends in the community, and who then as a secular priest had been Wiseman's very able Vicar-General. There were twelve clergy by 1880.[75] This had increased to seventeen by 1895.[76]

Notable among the more celebrated Jesuits at Farm Street was Fr Peter Gallwey[77] (Vice-Rector 1858–59, Rector 1860–69 and 1877–81, Provincial 1873–76; fig. 15), who in 1857 initiated the Sodality of the Immaculate Conception. This was intended primarily for the alumni of Jesuit schools, such as their former Stonyhurst pupil Lord Arundell,[78] with another such pupil, the Hon. Charles Langdale, as Treasurer. Again, the Sodality's membership drew on distinguished converts such as Newman's friend Serjeant Bellasis,[79] who had made a fortune as a legal expert on railways and urban water supplies, and who was received with his family by Fr Brownbill in 1850. Another such was Lord Walter Kerr,[80] later First Naval Lord and Admiral, who became a Catholic as a boy following his mother, the Marchioness of Lothian. The Sodality met in the Jesuit house on a weekly basis to sing the Office of Our Lady.

Another of the Farm Street clergy's chief functions was as convert-makers, a thousand converts having been received, it is said, in its first eighteen years, as 'a clinic for those with Roman tendencies'.[81] But the converts' register begins only in 1862, so no record exists of the reception of some of the most notable, who included, on Passion Sunday 1851, William Ewart Gladstone's closest friends, his 'two eyes', the future Cardinal Henry Edward Manning (fig. 16) and the lawyer James Hope,[82] who became Hope-Scott and the heir of Sir Walter Scott's house and estate of Abbotsford; Hope-Scott also made a fortune from the railways. John Henry Newman (fig. 17) preached the panegyric in the church at Hope-Scott's requiem. Manning was received by Fr Brownbill, moving 'silently out of the ranks to perform his one historic action', according to the patronising Shane Leslie,[83] who overlooked Brownbill's other converts; Wiseman and others seem to have regarded him as a safe pair of hands with distinguished Anglicans. Manning celebrated his first Mass in the church (sketched by Dicky Doyle) on 16 June 1851, he said Mass and had a confessional there on his visits to London from Rome, and, on his return to reside in England, he lived nearby with his deceased wife's aunt at 78 Audley Street between 1854 and 1856. In his own words, Manning 'made some inconvenience in the Church',[84] he thought from the numbers whom he attracted as penitents and converts, and his link with Farm Street was severed. From 1857 he was busy elsewhere as Provost of the Westminster Chapter, with his own Bayswater parish of St Mary of the Angels and his new diocesan order of St Charles Borromeo.

Manning came to deplore what he saw as the 'exclusive, narrow, military, aristocratic, character of the Society ... [which] seems to me to be a mysterious permission of God for the chastisement of England'.[85] He thought that the Jesuits showed contempt for their fellow priests,

and that they flourished at the expense of the wider Church.[86] He assured the rejection of the Jesuit plan for a house and school in Westminster, for which they had land given by his friend James Hope-Scott. He had a particular dislike of three Jesuits, Lythgoe, Gallwey and Fr Alfred Weld, the last discussed below, and he became a strong critic of the Society, securing from Rome the Constitution *Romanos Pontifices* (1881), which brought the religious orders, the Jesuits especially, more effectively under episcopal control. The Society accepted that the definite arrangements of the Constitution removed grounds for conflict. Manning himself maintained a ban in his archdiocese on the opening of a Jesuit secondary school. The establishment of St Ignatius College, Stamford Hill, came only in 1894, after his death.

Cecil, Dowager Marchioness of Lothian (fig. 19),[87] followed Manning into the Church at Farm Street in June 1851; Charlotte, Duchess of Buccleuch,[88] formerly Mistress of the Robes to Queen Victoria, in 1860. Other notable converts included Frances Taylor,[89] a journalist and novelist and the founding co-editor in 1864 of the Jesuit journal *The Month*; she had been received into the church by a Jesuit, Fr Woollett,[90] while nursing wounded soldiers in the Crimea in 1855. She came under the direction of the effective and charismatic Fr James Clare (Rector 1871–77),[91] who was popular as a missioner among the poor by appearing to be Irish, although he was in fact Lancastrian. As Mother Mary Magdalen (fig. 20), Frances Taylor became the foundress in 1872 of the Poor Servants of the Mother of God, for girls without dowries, which moved to Mount Street. Her subsequent spiritual director was the Jesuit Fr Augustus Dignam,[92] who joined with her to write her new Order's Ignatian rule and constitutions. Despite some Jesuit reservations in the matter, she was also to write his memoir and publish his *Conferences* (*c*. 1897) and *Retreats* (1896–98).[93] Janet Erskine Stuart,[94] a hard-riding young horsewoman and huntswoman connected to the convert Earl of Gainsborough and his family, was received at the church in 1879, and was wisely guided by Gallwey in an extant correspondence,[95] later becoming Mother General of the Sacred Heart Sisters, and developing her order's distinctive philosophy of education. Another associate of the church, from 1869, was Mary Elizabeth Towneley (fig. 21), descended from the Old Catholic Towneley and Tichborne families. She was a member of Fr Clare's Confraternity of the Sacred Heart, and ultimately became Provincial of the Sisters of Notre-Dame de Namur.[96] The novelists Lady Georgiana Fullerton,[97] grand-daughter of the Duke of Devonshire and the Marquess of Stafford, with family connections to six more dukes and three earls,[98] and John Oliver Hobbes (Mrs Craigie),[99] were also received into the Church, the first by Fr Brownbill in 1846, the second by Fr Michael Gavin[100] in 1892.

Peter Gallwey, 'a man of strong likes and dislikes … a man of quick temper',[101] was also the spiritual director of Frances Taylor and her close friend Lady Georgiana Fullerton. Inspired in part by a humble capmaker, Elisabeth Twiddy, Gallwey and Fullerton created the Immaculate Conception Charity for the rescue of orphans, which conducted a wildly successful charitable

Fig. 22
Lady Georgiana
Fullerton's memorial
plaque at Farm Street

bazaar in 1861, at St James's Hall, Piccadilly, raising £6,000, with donations from the Pope, the Empresses of Austria, France and Brazil, the Queen of Spain and the King of the Belgians. It was later complained that the money raised was dissipated among too many objects instead of the intended single orphanage.[102] Gallwey was also chiefly responsible for founding in 1905 and funding St Joseph's Hospice for the Dying in Hackney, which he staffed with Irish Sisters of Charity.[103] Lady Georgiana Fullerton is commemorated in the church by a plaque (fig. 22) and by the north window. She and her husband suffered greatly from the death of their only son, and she was closely associated with Frances Taylor in founding her order.

Perhaps more striking still was the influence of the Oxford Movement within the Church of England in producing converts to Rome, who then became distinguished members of the Society itself. The Farm Street community included Fr Albany Christie,[104] who had joined Newman at his retreat at Littlemore; Fr Frederick Hathaway, former Dean of Worcester College, Oxford;[105] and Fr Henry James Coleridge,[106] a former Fellow of Oriel College, Oxford, the brother of the Chief Justice and the son of the judge Sir John Taylor Coleridge,[107] who had remarked on the moral deterioration of converts at Newman's trial for libelling the promiscuous renegade Italian Dominican Fr Giacinto Achilli. Coleridge was Newman's closest friend in the Society. On taking over the Jesuit journal *The Month* in 1865 from Frances Taylor, its founding co-editor, he printed Newman's *The Dream of Gerontius* in its May and June issues. *The Month* was to become the major outlet for Jesuit publication. In 1877 Coleridge also became editor of another Jesuit periodical, the devotional *The Messenger of the Sacred Heart*. He was a prolific writer, best known for his eighteen-volume life of Our Lord (*The Life of Our Life*, 1876–92) and for his Quarterly Series of red-bound volumes of theology, history and biography, for which he wrote and edited the lives and letters of St Francis Xavier (1881) and St Teresa of Avila (2 vols, 1881–96), and of contemporary figures such as Lady Georgiana Fullerton.[108] Another convert, the Cambridge historian Fr John Morris (fig. 23),[109] had been a Canon of Northampton and then Westminster, and secretary to Cardinal Wiseman and then to Manning, before becoming a Jesuit. He was Postulator of the Cause of the English Martyrs, and wrote lives of St Thomas Becket (1859 and 1885) and the Jesuit martyr John Gerard (1881), and *The Troubles of Our Catholic Forefathers* (3 vols, 1872–77). He died in the pulpit at Wimbledon.

The distinguished historian Joseph Stevenson[110] became a Jesuit at the age of 71 and lived at Farm Street between 1881 and 1895. Stevenson was a former married man, a Presbyterian and librarian to the Dean and Chapter of Durham, then Anglican Vicar of Leighton Buzzard. He was received by Fr Gallwey in 1862, and later became a Catholic priest. He was one of the initiators of the Rolls Series of medieval British and Irish texts, with a lifelong achievement of more than fifty years of scholarship as a distinguished editor and translator, beginning in the 1830s and continuing until his death.[111]

Fig. 23
Fr John Morris, *c.* 1890s.
Photographer unknown

24

Fig. 24
Fr John Hungerford
Pollen, probably late 1890s.
Photographer unknown

Fig. 25
Fr Alfred Weld.
Photograph E. Fauries,
Poona and Bombay

Fig. 26
Fr Herbert Thurston.
Photographer unknown

Christie, Hathaway, Coleridge and Morris were born between 1814 and 1826 and died between 1890 and 1893, the long-lived Stevenson in 1895. They were part of the great gift of the Oxford Movement to the Roman Catholic Church in England.

Morris's successor as an expert on the English Martyrs and the Counter-Reformation was the Jesuit John Hungerford Pollen (fig. 24).[112] His father, an Oxford Movement convert of the same name,[113] had been Newman's Professor of Fine Art at the Catholic University of Ireland and was the architect of the neo-Byzantine University Church in Dublin.

A lay convert associated with the Society, the botanist James Britten (1846–1924), founded in 1884 the Catholic Truth Society, which was to become known to all Catholics for its pamphlets distributed through the churches. The Farm Street Jesuits housed the Society and made a major contribution to its work.

Fr Basset remarks that apart from Fr Waterworth, an historian of the Jesuit order (1852) and of relations between England and Rome (1854), 'the Province had produced no writer of distinction before 1864'. Then by blowing 'a metaphorical whistle', the Provincial, Fr Alfred Weld (fig. 25),[114] Manning's third dislike in the Society, and later the author of a learned work on the Society's suppression in Portugal, decided to make Farm Street the place for a scriptorium or House of Writers.[115] Coleridge and Morris were to become its directors, and it was to be distinguished by the community's greatest scholar of the next generation, the historian Fr Herbert Thurston (fig. 26), who published his first article in *The Month* in 1878, and came into permanent residence at Farm Street in 1894.[116] Fr Thurston's enormous output of learned essays, some 150 in the *Catholic Encyclopaedia* alone, includes the highly readable and sometimes sensational collection *No Popery: Chapters on Anti-Papal Prejudice*,[117] and two posthumously assembled volumes of essays exploring the wilder shores of Catholic religious experience, *The Physical Phenomena of Mysticism*[118] and *Surprising Mystics*.[119] Weld also established the internal *Letters and Notices*, beginning in 1862, containing much material on the Jesuit house itself.

The Jesuits' greatest individual failure was with the Irishman George Tyrrell (fig. 27),[120] who became Fr Christie's Catholic convert, aged only 18, at Farm Street, in 1879. Tyrrell joined the Society almost at once. As he laconically remarked, 'Here was post-haste and no mistake; from start to goal, from post to finish, in twenty-four hours. I had come out that afternoon with no intention of being received, and I returned a papist and half a Jesuit.'[121] He became a member of the House of Writers and befriended the Catholic biographer Wilfrid Ward and the late Victorian intellectual elite as a member of the Synthetic Society. Tyrrell was a literary and theological genius, with a bitter and biting wit, whose works are still read and readable, despite their dated Modernist programme, based upon a view of Christ as the spirit-filled if deluded prophet of an otherworldly kingdom that only came in the form of the Church. This could appear as Catholic apologetic, a neat inversion of Protestant expectations of the Gospel, as it was destructive of the project

Fig. 27
Fr George Tyrrell. Photographer unknown

of liberal Protestant scholars such as Adolf von Harnack and some of his fellow German professors to reconstruct a Christ who would be acceptable to the contemporary world as a teacher of modern morality. Tyrrell was dismissed from the Society in 1906, dying in 1909. He thought it 'good in its origin; beneficent in large tracts of its history,' and he continued to like some of its members, but he was also scathing about it, asserting that 'through arrested and distorted development and through lack of elasticity, [it] has grown out of harmony with a rapidly developing culture; and has thus become on the whole a source of discord and mischief; of a great deal more evil than good'.[122] Some of his brethren, such as Gallwey and Thurston, continued to hold him in affection, Gallwey expressing the view, the disgraced Tyrrell was told, that 'he has no fears for me'.[123]

As a fashionable church, Farm Street was touched by royalty. A requiem for the Prince Imperial, Louis Napoléon, was sung in 1879 after his killing by the Zulus (fig. 28); the Prince

Fig. 28
Queen Victoria and Princess Beatrice place wreathes at the coffin of the Prince Imperial, Louis Napoléon, at Camden Place, Chislehurst. A requiem for the prince was sung at Farm Street. *The Graphic*, 19 July 1879. Mary Evans Picture Library

Fig. 29
The Requiem Mass for the Archduke Rudolf of Austria, Crown-Prince of Austria-Hungary, at the Church of the Immaculate Conception, Farm Street, 1889. *The Graphic*, 9 February 1889. Mary Evans Picture Library

Fig. 30
The Empress Eugénie, flanked by Mme d'Attainville and M. Pietri, leaves the Church of the Immaculate Conception, Farm Street, after the requiem of Mme d'Arcos, 29 November 1913. Photograph from Edward Legge, *The Empress Eugénie and Her Son*, Dodd, Mead and Co., New York, 1916

of Wales attended the requiem for the Crown-Prince of Austria-Hungary, Rudolf, in 1889 (fig. 29); and the church was attended by Prince Carlos of Portugal,[124] who, as King Carlos, was assassinated with his elder son in 1908.[125] Another attender, in November 1913, was the Archduke Franz Ferdinand with his wife, both assassinated in 1914 at Sarajevo. In the same year the ex-Empress Eugénie and the Queen of Spain attended the requiem at Farm Street of their friend Mme d'Arcos (fig. 30).

The insecurities of late Victorian society, even for the comfortable, are suggested by the story of Belinda Murphy, mistress of the Mount Loftus estate at Powerstown in Ireland. She was coming out of the church early on Sunday 17 December 1899, when she 'met a news-boy shouting awful battle hundreds killed & wounded' at Colenso in South Africa. 'She bought a paper and the very first name that she saw, in the list of those killed, was her eldest son.'[126] The church's military connections are supremely represented by the memorial to its devoted attender Sir Luke O'Connor VC KCB (figs 31, 32), who in 1857 was invested with the Victoria Cross.[127] His gallant action on 20 September 1854 at the Battle of the Alma in the Crimea was the first for which the award was made to the Army. His citation also refers to his gallantry at Sevastopol on 8 September 1855, when he was wounded through both thighs. O'Connor was born in County Roscommon. His father died of cholera when the family was on ship to Canada in 1839, and his mother and brother died of smallpox after arriving in Quebec. Brought up by relations on his return to Ireland, he enlisted as a Private in the Royal Welch Fusiliers and later served during the Indian Mutiny and Ashanti War; he retired as an honorary Major-General. His medals were at one time displayed in the church.

Farm Street did not only minister to the great and good. A striking aspect of Gallwey's memorial orations was his theme of the supreme spiritual value of generosity to the poor and of Holy Poverty. This, of course, had a real significance for the religious, and some of Gallwey's following like Lady Georgiana Fullerton placed a particular emphasis upon it in the severity and self-denial of their private lives, which stand in dramatic contrast to their wealth and social position.[128] Fullerton was at the centre of a circle of great ladies known for their piety and charity who were encouraged by the Jesuits themselves.[129] One member of the community, Fr Frederick Hathaway (fig. 33), who had practised the severest forms of self-denial as an Anglican, ministered to the poor at Horseferry Road, and was always careful to work into an address to an Irish audience the sentence 'When I was last in Tipperary'.[130] He 'did not believe that any poor man could commit more than a venial sin'.[131] The Society's principal contact with the poor came in the parish missions that its members preached throughout England every year. Its concern with the poor lacked the sense of social justice of the more modern Jesuit social programme associated with Fr Charles Plater,[132] founder of the Catholic Social Guild, who was not himself a member of the Farm Street community.[133]

Fig. 31
Louis William Desanges,
*Sergeant Luke O'Connor
Winning His VC at the Battle of
the Alma, 20 September 1854,*
undated. Oil on canvas,
65 x 78 cm. Royal Welch
Fusiliers Regimental Museum,
Caernarfon Castle, 4033

Fig. 32
Memorial in the church to
Sir Luke O'Connor VC KCB

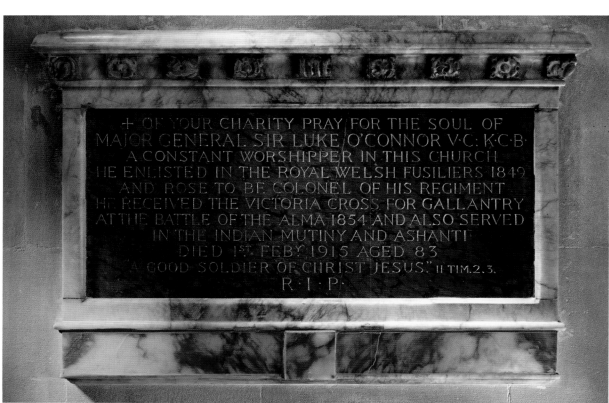

Fig. 33
Fr Frederick Hathaway, *c.* 1864–69.
Photograph George Heron Hay,
191 Regent Street

Fig. 34
'Spy' (Leslie Ward), 'Fr Bernard
John Vaughan', *Vanity Fair*,
30 January 1907. Mary Evans
Picture Library

Fig. 35
Fr Cyril Martindale, *c.* 1940s.
Photographer unknown

Plater was anticipated in a more sensational if less sophisticated manner by Fr Bernard Vaughan (fig. 34),[134] who was brother to the Cardinal, an Archbishop and an Abbot, and five nun sisters. Vaughan packed Farm Street Sunday by Sunday in 1906 with his sermons against the 'Smart Set' and its fashionable vices, from marital infidelity and the arrangement of marriages to heiresses to cheating dressmakers. The sermons were published as *The Sins of Society*, which then went through fourteen editions;[135] 'the congregation thronged the nave and aisles, overflowed into the chapels, sat on altar-rails or pillar pedestals, and was marshalled into queues outside by policemen who regretted their Sunday rest.'[136] Vaughan was alleged to have outraged London clubland by rebuking gambling and to have spoiled the three-month season, which he described 'as a three-act drama which, if it did not turn out to be but a bad farce, ended as tragedy'.[137] He was a simple and prayerful priest but also a showman of genius, immensely popular in the East End as a missioner, and was never happier than when preaching from a tabletop with a bell and crucifix in the rough courts of the poor, mobbed by small ragged girls and boys, and providing them with boots and a hall for entertainment.[138] Vaughan's biographer Fr Cyril Martindale (fig. 35)[139] carried the tradition of Jesuit writers long into the twentieth century.

Manning's and Tyrrell's objections to the Society suggest that it was a semi-military body that imposed a mental and moral straitjacket on its members – in a spirit, paradoxically, not unlike Manning's own. This hardly corresponds to the able, vigorous and energetic characters of some of the priests described here, although Jesuits might sometimes rejoice in the military metaphor. Thus Fr John Morris was said to have had 'a very intense military spirit. He was a soldier by nature, and he rejoiced – we might almost say revelled – in the military spirit of blind obedience that the Society of Jesus inculcates in her sons.'[140] The paradox was that this very spirit could intensify a radical individualism, as it did with Morris himself. Yet Jesuit obituaries often dwelt upon the gentler qualities of their subjects, as in that of Fr James Clare, which stressed his 'innate kindness and sympathy', his helpfulness in difficulties, his ready emotion, affectionateness and warm-heartedness, even if this meant 'promising perhaps to do more than he could accomplish'.[141]

Yet hostile criticism was a backhanded compliment, an acknowledgement of the success of the Society in doing very well whatever it tried to do well. Farm Street is the monument to that success.

MICHAEL HALL

THE ARCHITECTURE AND FURNISHINGS OF THE CHURCH AND THE ASSOCIATED BUILDINGS IN FARM STREET AND MOUNT STREET

In 1903 the Jesuits' Church of the Immaculate Conception was finally completed by the construction of its west aisle, fifty-four years after the building had been formally opened. In its review of the new addition, *The Tablet* noted that the aisle had been designed by 'the fourth firm of architects to have a hand in the structure, which is so far composite, after the manner of the early church-makers'.[1] As this suggests, very few Victorian churches have such a complicated building history. There are several reasons for this. Built in four principal phases, the church's evolution reflects the growth of its congregation and the burgeoning support for its clergy in the second half of the nineteenth century. Each advance in construction or decoration involved the appointment of a new architect, partly reflecting changing fashions. However, the most important reason why the story is so complex – and occasionally obscure – is simply that the site itself imposed slow and unpredictable progress on the building's development.

FINDING A SITE

Active discussions about fundraising for a church for the Jesuits in central London were underway by the autumn of 1836. The possibility became concrete in 1839 thanks to an anonymous donation of £700 to Fr John Bird, the Provincial, 'towards building a Church in London to be dedicated to the Ever Immaculate Blessed Virgin and to be called "The Immaculate Conception"' (see fig. 3).[2] This prompted Fr Randall Lythgoe (1793–1855), the Jesuit who had most energetically promoted the idea, to seek advice from Fr Thomas Glover, an English Jesuit in Rome.

'No time is to be lost in making a beginning of a church and house in London,' replied Glover briskly:

> Now the way to proceed is this: in the first place look out for, and purchase, an eligible situation for a large church and house ... When you have secured the ground, you tell the bishop, that you are going to build ... and hope that he will give his blessing to the undertaking ... The ground should be freehold if possible, or at least on a lease with a small quit rent for 900 years or so ... Let the plan be well considered beforehand, never depart from it, think only of getting the walls up, and well covered in, the ornamental parts may be deferred to your successors. No great church was ever built and furnished in one generation.[3]

There were several problems to be overcome. First, Thomas Griffiths, the bishop – or Vicar Apostolic as the post was known before the re-establishment of the Catholic hierarchy in England in 1850 – was not at all inclined to give his permission, since he feared that the Jesuits would attract support at the expense of his own churches. He tried to elbow them out of the way by offering a site for a new church at, among other places, Bethnal Green, which, as Lythgoe

Fig. 36
Our Lady of Farm Street, at the south-east corner of the chancel, was presented to the church in 1868. Carved and painted by the Munich firm of ecclesiastical decorators Mayer & Co., the statue stands under a canopy designed by Fr Ignatius Scoles, son of the church's first architect.

Fig. 37
A sketch plan of the site of the church
when the Jesuits acquired their lease in 1841.
It lies between Farm Street, on the left,
and what were then the grounds of the
St George's parish workhouse on the right.
The parts shown without hatching (occupied
by stables) did not become available until
several years later, meaning that the church
had to be built in stages.

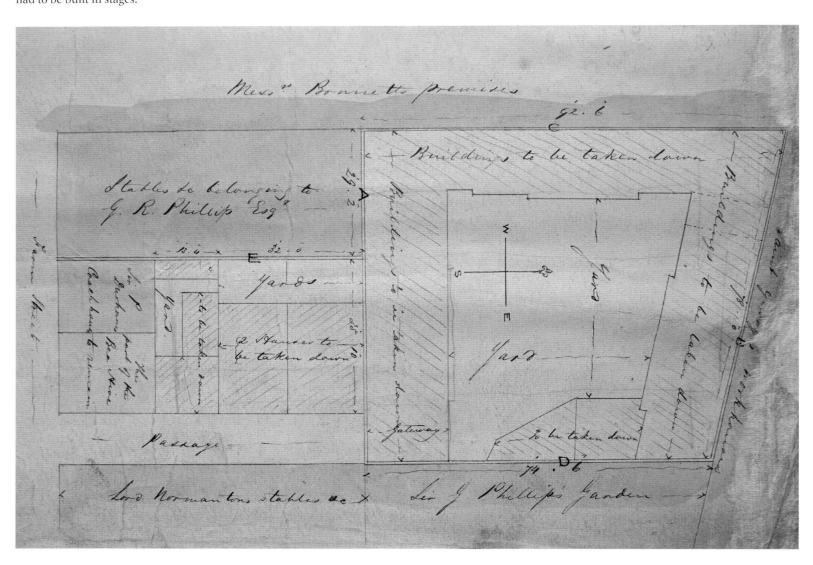

wrote in contempt to Glover, 'is out of London, little if any short of four miles from any Govt. offices, a situation where the Society wd have been perfectly buried'.[4] Lythgoe was determined to have the Jesuits at the centre of London, but he recognised that he could expect neither episcopal approval nor substantial subscriptions for a new church until he had found somewhere to build it. It was not until April 1841 that he was able to write to Glover: 'I have it in my power at this moment to purchase a leasehold site in the very middle of St Georges [Hanover Square] Parish ... but Fr Bird thinks it not large enough, though a Church could be built upon it at small cost, larger or as large as any of the existing [Roman Catholic] Chapels, except Moorfields.'[5]

Lythgoe managed to overcome Bird's reservations, but the site (fig. 37) was undeniably unpromising. Tucked away on Farm Street, it occupied a mews area serving the town houses in Berkeley Square to the east and Grosvenor Square to the north. A rectangle, orientated north–south, it consisted of a stable yard filling the whole of the northern part, which was separated from Mount Street to the north by the St George's parish workhouse. A number of smaller stable buildings and coach houses extended south towards Farm Street, two of which were not included in the lease. The property was part of the Berkeley Estate, and since William Berkeley, Lord Segrave, raised no objection to a Roman Catholic place of worship being built on his land, the site was let for 99 years to the Jesuits for £5,856. An agreement was brokered in Rome between the Order and the Vicar Apostolic: in return for Griffiths allowing building to go ahead, the Jesuits agreed that their church would not have parochial status – meaning that baptisms, marriages and funerals could not take place there, and other Catholic churches in central London would not, therefore, be deprived of the revenues that such services produced.[6]

CHOOSING AN ARCHITECT

Lythgoe succeeded Bird as Provincial in 1841, and set about fundraising in earnest, with rapid success. The subscriptions book for the new church was opened in January 1842 with contributions from many of the country's leading Catholic families, headed by £500 from Sir Charles Tempest. By the end of 1845, when work on the church was well underway, £4,445 had been subscribed, with another £1,080 promised.[7] This latter sum included £500 pledged by a prominent Catholic nobleman, the 16th Earl of Shrewsbury, but Lythgoe was apprehensive that the promise came with strings, writing in 1840 that 'Lord S. used to say that he would do something handsome, but unless *Pugin* is to be appointed architect he may not be inclined to do much.'[8] Shrewsbury was the most significant lay patron of the most celebrated Catholic architect in Britain, A. W. N. Pugin, whom he had commissioned to remodel his family seat, Alton Towers in Staffordshire; he also paid for Pugin's most famous church, St Giles, Cheadle, opened in the autumn of 1846. However, by the time Lythgoe laid the foundation stone of the Church of the Immaculate Conception on 31 July 1844, he had already appointed J. J. Scoles as architect,

Fig. 38
'Church of the Immaculate Conception,
Farm Street, Berkeley Square. W.'
Plan by A. T. Perrin for Williams and
Winkley Architects, 1966. ABSI, PC/1/2/16

necessitating a diplomatic passage in the letter that Lythgoe wrote to Lord Shrewsbury to remind him about the £500:

> *Your Lordship would have wished that Pugin had been employed – Personally, I should not have had an objection, but the Church had been partly promised to Scoles & then there are many who object to Mr Pugin, that he is expensive & that he will not allow any competition. I know it is more convenient for him to employ one Builder but People generally do not like it – of Pugin's great Talents there can be no doubt, especially for everything connected with decoration.*[9]

Despite Lythgoe's objection to Pugin's preference always to use one trusted builder – George Myers, based in Southwark – rather than put work out to tender, the main explanation for the choice of architect must be that Scoles had a long record of working for the Jesuits, and that Lythgoe wanted to employ an architect whom he knew. In the event, Shrewsbury raised no objection to his favourite architect not being used, and paid the £500. Pugin was, however, to make a significant contribution to Scoles's church.

Born in London in 1798, Joseph John Scoles was forty-six and at the peak of his career when he received the commission for the Church of the Immaculate Conception.[10] Catholic by birth – he was the son of a London joiner – he had been articled to the leading Catholic architect of the time, Joseph Ireland, a relative of his mother. Ireland designed Gothic as well as classical buildings and as a pupil Scoles demonstrated a strong interest in medieval ecclesiastical architecture. By the 1840s he was known principally as a designer of Roman Catholic churches, and although the majority were Gothic he did not share Pugin's belief that this was the sole permissible style: he designed a number of Romanesque churches, and his best-known building after the Immaculate Conception, the chapel at Prior Park College, Bath, begun in 1844, is classical, in keeping with the Palladian style of the college's other buildings.

DESIGNING THE CHURCH

The English Jesuits were undoctrinaire in matters of architectural style. This was in contrast to the Oratorians, who under the leadership of John Henry Newman, rejected Gothic for new buildings on the grounds that as a Counter-Reformation order they had no medieval past, and the style was therefore of no contemporary relevance to them. One reason why the Jesuits did not follow suit may be that their first headquarters in England, Stonyhurst in Lancashire – where they established a school in 1794 (fig. 14) – is an Elizabethan mansion. When in 1832 Scoles added a church, St Peter, he chose a Perpendicular Gothic style to be in keeping with the house. Although Scoles's first building for the Jesuits, St Winefride, Holywell, Flintshire

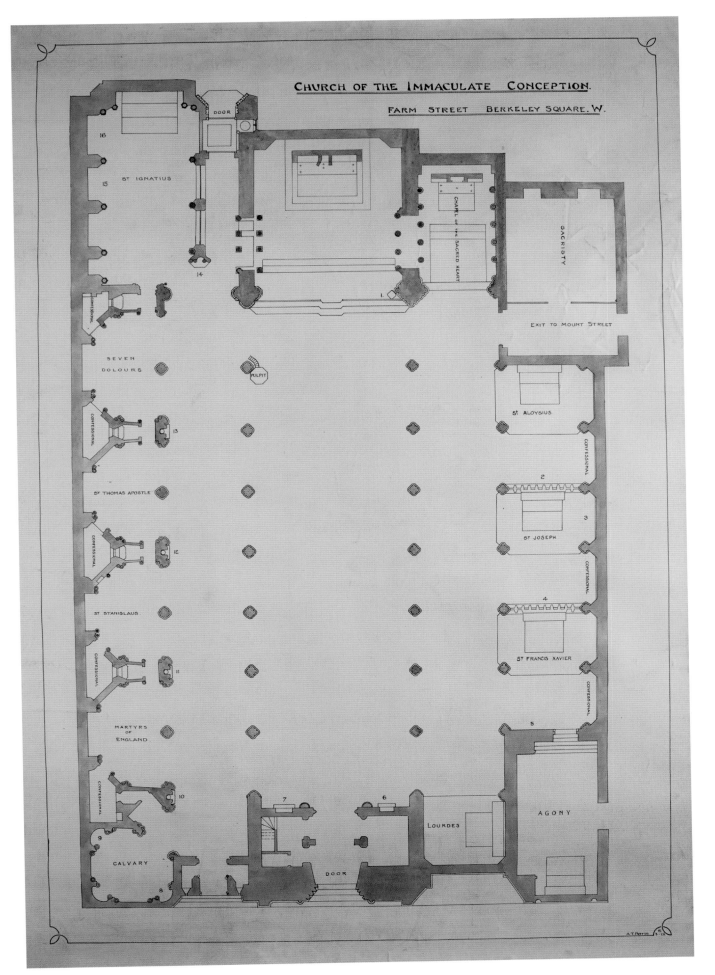

CHURCH OF THE IMMACULATE CONCEPTION.

FARM STREET BERKELEY SQUARE. W.

Church of the Immaculate Conception,
FARM STREET, BERKELEY SQUARE.

Foundation Stone laid on the 31st of July, 1844.   The Church opened on the 31st of July, 1849.
J. J. SCOLES, Esq., Architect.

[From The Builder, June 2, 1849.]

Fig. 39
This engraving by C. D. Laing of the church's
south front, on Farm Street, was first
published in *The Builder* in 1849, to mark
the opening of the church. On the left are
stables and on the right is the truncated
east aisle, which had its own door.

(1832–33), was classical, his subsequent churches for them were Gothic, including St Ignatius, Preston (1833–36), and St Francis Xavier, Liverpool (1845–48). Scoles touchingly demonstrated his loyalty and gratitude to the Jesuits by naming his eldest son 'Ignatius' after the order's founder, St Ignatius of Loyola: having been trained as an architect by his father, Ignatius Scoles was ordained and became a Jesuit. He was to make a small contribution to his father's church in the form of the lofty canopy over the large statue of Our Lady of Farm Street at the south-east corner of the chancel (see fig. 36).

Lythgoe was the priest in charge at St Winefride at the time Scoles's church was being built, and this may have been the origin of their friendship. He was probably behind the choice of Scoles to design the architect's first London church, Our Lady, St John's Wood, opened in 1836 and intended for the Jesuits, although never in the end conveyed to them. Before it was completed, Lythgoe showed this church to Pugin, who hated it: 'a more flimsey [*sic*] lath & plaister concern I never beheld. there is not a single bit of substantial construction about it ... modern) modern) modern) bad) bad) bad)'.[11] Ten years later, Scoles's churches could not be criticised as 'flimsey'. Both the Immaculate Conception and St Francis Xavier – a church that Scoles may also have owed to Lythgoe, who founded the attached college in 1842 – are mature and solid expressions of the mid-nineteenth-century Gothic revival ideal as formulated by not only Pugin but also such Anglican architects as R. C. Carpenter and George Gilbert Scott.

The constraints of the site at Farm Street meant that the church could not be conventionally orientated. The liturgical east end faces north, giving the interior the cool, even light that is such an important part of its character. Scoles designed double aisles to the nave, the inner ones for congregational seating and the outer ones for chapels. The intrusion into the southern part of the site of buildings that were not included in the Jesuits' lease meant that initially there was space to build the aisles along only the three northern bays of the nave, which extended south towards Farm Street for another five aisleless bays. Since the building was so tightly hemmed in by stables and coach houses, Scoles gave the church a tall clerestory and large windows at both north and south ends to ensure that it would be adequately lit. When the church was completed, the only major part clearly visible to the public was the south front, on Farm Street, and so Scoles concentrated the building's external display there (fig. 39). A doorway under a steep, traceried gable, flanked by gabled image niches, is set below a large window that incorporates a rose of Flamboyant French type. There was a smaller rose in the gable, and the front is flanked by thick buttresses that rise to elaborately pinnacled turrets. The principal source for the composition is the upper part of the south transept of Beauvais Cathedral, designed by Martin Chambiges and built in 1500–50. Scoles's reworking on a small scale of this vast composition is strikingly successful, and in some ways more aesthetically coherent than its model.

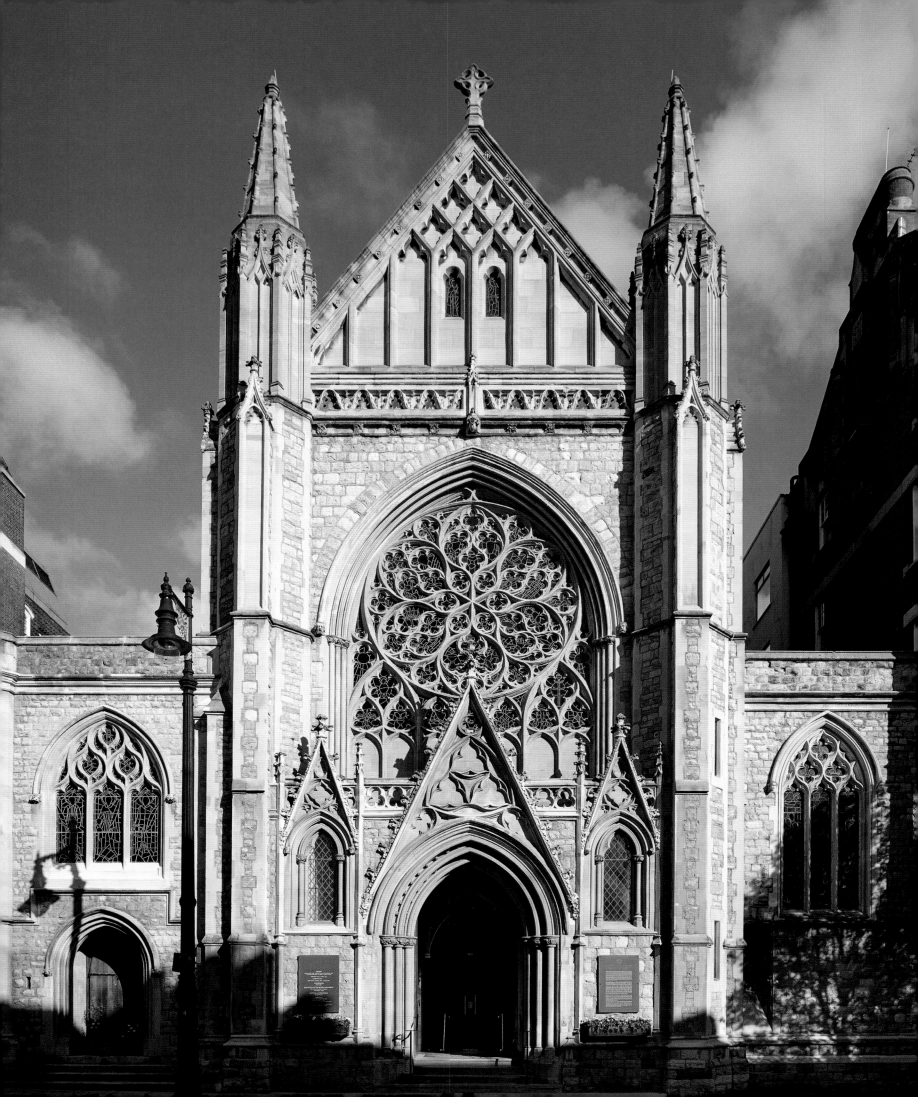

Fig. 40
The south front as it appears today.
Comparison with the engraving illustrated
on page 36 reveals the complexity of the
history of this apparently uniform façade.
The east aisle, on the right, was completed
in 1878; the west aisle, on the left, was not
finished until 1903. In 1951, following war
damage, the nave's gable was reconstructed
to his own design by Adrian Gilbert Scott.

Like the rest of Scoles's exterior, the south front is faced with Kentish Rag, with Box stone (from Wiltshire) for the architectural detail. Rag is a bluish-grey limestone from the vicinity of Maidstone that was much liked in the 1840s because it was finished with a rough face that gives buildings a picturesquely textured surface. Unfortunately, that quality also attracts soot, which later both blackened the stone and led to its decay. It was not used by subsequent architects who worked on the church, who preferred the smooth surface of cream-coloured Bath stone. As early as the 1880s, by which time the south front was only just over thirty years old, much of the detail of the upper part of the façade was in such poor condition that it had to be completely replaced by George Goldie.[12] After serious damage to the church in the Second World War (see below) the gable was rebuilt in simpler form (fig. 40), with blind niches replacing the rose – a detail that brings the composition even closer to its model at Beauvais.

The best record of the entrance front's original appearance is the engraving published in *The Builder* in 1849 (fig. 39) to mark the opening of the church. To the left of the façade can be seen the coach house that had prevented the west aisle being continued the full length of the nave; on the right is the temporary south wall of the east aisle, which was not to be extended further south until 1876–78, after the buildings – described as 'cottages' – on the very far right had been acquired by the Jesuits and demolished. One element proposed by Scoles was never built: he envisaged the west aisle terminating on the street with a tower, presumably for bells.[13]

By contrast to the elaborate composition of the entrance front, the north front (fig. 41) is little more than a large nine-light window modelled closely on the east window of Carlisle Cathedral, a spectacular exercise in Decorated tracery completed in 1340. In the interior, this window is the feature that principally justifies Lythgoe's comment on Scoles's design, writing to the Earl of Shrewsbury in 1844: 'I flatter myself that your Ldp will be pleased with it. It will be, *not a Barn*, but in the *Decorated Style*.'[14] This was a more loaded remark than is now apparent. Following Emancipation in 1829, the need to build churches for a Catholic population that was growing rapidly thanks principally to immigration from Ireland meant an emphasis on large and often underfunded buildings that were readily compared to 'barns' thanks to their lack of decoration. However, there was a more significant reason behind the comparison. The English were not used to churches designed to obey the principles of liturgical planning enforced after the Counter-Reformation. A new emphasis on lay participation in the Mass had led to a break with medieval precedent in the requirement for wide and shallow sanctuaries, with no chancel screens, to allow the congregation an uninterrupted view of the altar not only for the Mass itself but also for Benediction, a rite that assumed a new importance from the sixteenth century onwards. This resulted in spacious, open interiors on the model of the Jesuits' church in Rome, the Gesù, consecrated in 1584, which influentially abandoned nave aisles altogether in the interests of not only visibility but also audibility, since preaching was an important part of the Jesuits' mission.

Fig. 41
The north front of the church, seen across Mount Street Gardens. This façade was originally largely invisible to the public, as it backed onto the workhouse of the parish of St George, Hanover Square. The workhouse was demolished in 1885.

This was a problem for Gothic-revival architects such as Pugin, for whom medieval churches were the ideal. Pugin publicly challenged Counter-Reformation principles in his attack on St John the Evangelist, Duncan Terrace, in Islington, an aisleless Romanesque design by Scoles, opened in 1843. In an article published in the *Dublin Review* and reprinted in his 1843 book *On the Present State of Ecclesiastical Architecture in England* Pugin deplored Scoles's refusal to follow 'ancient Catholic examples' in favour of 'modern experiments in ecclesiastical architecture' and in an engraving demonstrated how the site could easily have accommodated an aisled church of medieval form. Both Scoles and Lythgoe must have been aware of this criticism, which was published only a year before the commission for the Immaculate Conception. Lythgoe's promise that his new church would not be a 'barn' suggests that Pugin influenced the convincing way that at Farm Street Scoles fused the requirements of modern Catholic worship – principally a relatively shallow, broad chancel as wide as the nave – with aisles in the medieval manner, all as carefully detailed in the mid-fourteenth-century English Decorated style as any of Pugin's own churches – but without the chancel screen that Pugin urged was essential.

FURNISHING AND DECORATING SCOLES'S CHURCH

The only surviving letter from Scoles to Lythgoe concerning the church's design, sent in September 1844, just as the foundations were being completed, reveals that his first proposals had been enlarged and elaborated before work began. This was partly in order to accommodate the Jesuits' wishes: for example, Scoles raised the roofs of the nave aisles seven feet 'to get height for an organ gallery' at the south end, and greatly enlarged the sacristy. He also wrote that he had added 'decoration to the upper part of the Exterior viz. ornamental parapet Belfry Gable windows &c arising from these parts being visible which then not supposed would be so until the old buildings were cleared away'.[15] In April 1844, before the church had been begun, and probably as an aid to fundraising, Lythgoe commissioned a print (fig. 42) that is the only representation of Scoles's original design, since his drawings have been lost. Often misdated to 1849, after the church was completed, and criticised therefore as inaccurate, the print reveals that before work began Scoles made the major change of giving the roof a much steeper profile, avoiding the late medieval flat, panelled effect he had originally intended.[16] This change may have been connected with the raising of the nave aisle roofs necessitated by the decision to incorporate an organ gallery. Scoles also altered the design of the clerestory windows, substituting a low blind arcade for the blind lights below a transom shown in the print. Only the three aisle bays that could actually be built initially are represented. The print does not show the part of the outer west aisle that was constructed in this initial phase, but survey drawings made in the 1860s reveal that it contained confessionals, but no chapels. The nave is shown without benches, probably in order to allow the design to be appreciated more easily, but it

Fig. 42
A print of J. J. Scoles's design for the church, published in 1846 as an aid for fundraising. Scoles changed the design before work began by heightening the nave roof, which was given a much steeper pitch, probably so that the organ could be better accommodated. He also gave the aisles pitched roofs rather than the lean-tos shown here. The elaborate screen in front of what was to become the Sacred Heart Chapel, to the right of the chancel, was probably not executed. The print shows how Scoles intended to fit out the chancel, but in the event the high altar was designed by A. W. N. Pugin.

Fig. 43 (overleaf)
A general view of the church looking north. None of the decoration dates from Scoles's time. The painting of the Virgin Mary flanked by angels on the chancel arch was probably carried out in 1903 and the nave roof was painted to a design by Austin Winkley in 1987. The mosaic roundels in the spandrels of the nave arcades, which spell out the 'Ave Maria', were made in 1996 by Filomena Monteiro.

Fig. 44 (pages 46–47)
The chancel. Although its furnishings are the work of several designers over a long period, it makes a unified effect. The high altar was designed by A. W. N. Pugin in 1846; the chancel walls were lined with alabaster and marble in the 1860s, and in 1875 Salviati of Venice inserted the two mosaics on the north wall. The marble chancel rail, which incorporates panels of lapis lazuli, was designed by W. H. Romaine-Walker and installed in 1901.

is possible that it had not then been decided whether the church would be furnished with benches or chairs.

The chancel is flanked by two chapels, that of St Ignatius to the left and what was then the Blessed Sacrament Chapel to the right, which was to be approached through an elaborate screen (if this was in fact installed it did not survive the fire that gutted the chapel a decade after the opening of the church). The print suggests one element that was especially noted when the church opened: the painted decoration of the roof and walls by Henry Taylor Bulmer (1811–1857), a Roman Catholic artist who specialised in church work. According to the *Morning Post*'s description of the church after its opening in 1849, the sanctuary was 'a marvel of decoration' and the roof 'with its blue and gold, has the effect as it were of stars'.[17] Bulmer's work has been obliterated by war damage and subsequent repainting, but something of the impact of his scheme can be experienced in the nave of St Barnabas, Pimlico, where much of his decoration, dating from 1849–50, survives. Apart from the glazing of the tracery in the clerestory, Farm Street's original stained glass has also gone. There were windows by James Powell and Sons and Claudet and Houghton, based in High Holborn, but these were outshone by the glazing of the south rose, the great north window (a Tree of Jesse) and the clerestory, filled with 'small angelic figures in medallions … upon a ground of flowered quarries'.[18] All these latter windows were by William Wailes of Newcastle-upon-Tyne, probably at this date the best-known stained-glass maker in Britain (Wailes made all Pugin's glass from 1842 to 1845 and his work remained Puginian in style after that). Greatly admired when the church was opened – *The Illustrated London News* called the north window 'a masterpiece' – at £985 14s 8d these windows were also very expensive.[19]

In the 1844 print Scoles suggested what the high altar might look like: surmounted by a tabernacle and Benediction throne, enclosed on three sides by dossal curtains and flanked by niches containing sculpture. The actual, much more elaborate, high altar was designed by Pugin in 1846, and was paid for by Monica Tempest (1806–1860), whose family were such generous donors to the building fund: 'it will make a most glorious altar if carried out', wrote Pugin to Miss Tempest's brother Joseph, who dealt with the commission on her behalf, 'but I fear it is too good for Father Lythgoe's views'.[20] It is not clear what Lythgoe's objections might have been, since although the altar is medieval in its detailing, in design Pugin adhered to modern Roman Catholic requirements by making it tall and upright, to allow for a high Benediction throne over the tabernacle. It incorporates a rich array of sculpture (fig. 44): the front of the altar represents the Crucifixion, flanked by Old Testament types of Christ's sacrifice: Abel, Noah, Melchizedek and Abraham. The reredos represents the twenty-four Elders who surround the throne of Christ in heaven, as described in Revelation (4:10). There was no question of Pugin not being allowed to use his favourite craftsmen here: the altar, including all its

AVE MARIA
GRATIA
PLENA

Fig. 45
Three representations in the chancel of the
Virgin Mary crowned as Queen of Heaven:
in the statue of Our Lady of Farm Street,
in Salviati's mosaic and in Hardman's
north window.

sculpture, was made (of Caen stone) by George Myers, and the brass fittings are by Hardman of Birmingham. Pugin must have been pleased with the sculpture, since in 1848 he urged Lord Shrewsbury to go to see it in Myers's workshop.[21]

The opening of the Immaculate Conception on 31 July 1849 was widely and admiringly covered in the press. Scoles's design had already been noted when it was shown at the Royal Academy in 1847: *The Builder* commented that it was 'a clever design to which justice is scarcely done by the drawing'.[22] Even *The Ecclesiologist*, the polemical journal of the (Anglican) Ecclesiological Society, while decrying the exterior as 'decidedly too foreign and Flamboyant in character', grudgingly acknowledged that the design was 'laudable in conception as an attempt at a town church'.[23] Two years later, *The Builder* described the finished building as 'a very successful specimen of modern Gothic'.[24] Having commented that 'The situation of the new edifice, which has been for some years slowly and steadily rising, is not advantageous. The church stands in a mews', *The Morning Post* went on:

> *Very sacred associations, however, are attached to the humble idea of a stable; and if the locality be unfavourable, the extraordinary beauty of the building both externally and internally and especially in the latter respect, would more than efface any first impression of that kind.*[25]

The journalist concluded that 'the whole building is taken in at a glance. Nothing distracts the eye or breaks the effect.' This is still largely true today and it is a tribute to Scoles that even after the many additions to the church by other architects and the elaboration of both its furnishings and decoration, the spacious clarity of his original conception remains the dominant impression of the interior.

One implied additional reason why the church was admired from the outset was that it was evident that the Jesuits had not stinted on its cost. When asked by Lythgoe early in 1844 to estimate the likely sum needed to build the shell of the church, Scoles suggested around £4,500. Despite Lythgoe's objections to Pugin working always with a favoured builder, the contract was not put out to tender, but was offered to William Jackson of Brentford, presumably because Scoles knew him. Jackson's estimate was £5,008. Given the care with which Scoles enumerated the alterations to the initial design in order to justify to Lythgoe an increase of £500 over his informal estimate, it is all the more astonishing that Jackson's final charge was almost three times his estimate: £14,684. When other costs were added – including over £1,000 for the stained glass, £825 for the William Hill organ and £199 for the salary of Mr Tarrant, the clerk of works – the church had cost £19,628 by the time its fitting out was complete in 1851.[26] If Lythgoe ever objected to this steep rise in cost, it has left no trace in the records.

Fig. 46
The Sacred Heart Chapel. Designed by
Henry Clutton to replace a chapel gutted
by fire in 1859, it was the first major addition
to the church and is very different in style.
Inspired by French and Italian early Gothic
architecture, it reflects the influence of
John Ruskin's writings, notably *The Stones
of Venice* (1851–53). On the left-hand side
the wall arcade opens into the chancel.

Figs 47, 48 (overleaf and pages 54–55)
The rich furnishings of the Sacred Heart
Chapel include an altarpiece painted by
Peter Molitor and reliefs on the reredos and
altar front in gilt brass, made by Franchi
of Clerkenwell after models by Theodore
Phyffers, who also carved the demi-figures
of angels that line the walls. The marble
frieze of foliage behind them was
carved by Thomas Earp.

HENRY CLUTTON: THE SACRED HEART CHAPEL AND EAST AISLE

In 1859 the church narrowly escaped destruction when fire gutted the Blessed Sacrament Chapel, at the north end of the east aisle.[27] Lythgoe had died in 1855, which may be sufficient explanation why the commission for a replacement chapel – given a new dedication to the Sacred Heart – was not offered to Scoles, but the contrast between the style of the church and that of the new chapel is so strong that it may have been felt that he was too old-fashioned for the job. In the decade after the church opened there had been a revolution in Gothic-revival taste, partly in response to the writings of John Ruskin, who encouraged a move away from the fourteenth-century forms and painted decoration associated with Pugin towards early medieval sources – French as much as English – and the use of materials such as marble and granite to introduce colour. The Sacred Heart Chapel (fig. 46) is an exceptionally sumptuous and well-preserved exemplar of these new ideals.

Its architect was Henry Clutton (1819–1893), who had helped to pioneer the taste for early medieval French architecture when in 1856 he collaborated with William Burges on the winning entry for a competition to design a new cathedral at Lille. Although not built, their design in the early thirteenth-century French style made the two men's reputations, although it was almost immediately followed by a row that ended their partnership. Clutton's career took an unexpected turn when in 1857 he converted to Roman Catholicism. From then on he developed a practice as a church architect for Catholic clients with such success that in 1867 he was appointed architect for the proposed Westminster Cathedral. However, his design was abandoned in 1873 and the cathedral was eventually entrusted – after Clutton's death – to John Francis Bentley (1839–1902), who had been a pupil of Clutton from 1857 to 1860, when the Sacred Heart Chapel was being built.

The chapel is early French Gothic in style. Its pointed barrel-vaulted roof, of Caen stone, has cross ribs rising from a cornice richly carved with foliage by Thomas Earp (1828–1893), which is supported by marble columns. The upper walls are lined with polished alabaster inset with narrow patterned bands of marble. The north end is decorated with blind tracery, which forms a frame for a large three-panelled altar painting by the German artist Peter Molitor (1821–1898), depicting Christ displaying the Sacred Heart, flanked by the Virgin and saints.[28] At dado level the spandrels of the blind arcade on the chapel's flanking walls are filled with large alabaster demi-figures of angels (fig. 48) carved by Theodore Phyffers (c. 1821–1876). Born in Leuven, Phyffers had come to England in 1844 at Charles Barry's invitation to work on sculpture for the Houses of Parliament. He was also employed by Burges and was a close friend of Bentley, who is said to have designed the two small angels that flank the tabernacle.[29] In addition, Phyffers modelled the high-relief plaques on the reredos and front of the altar (depicting Joseph and his brethren; fig. 49), executed in electroplated brass by Franchi of Clerkenwell.[30]

Fig. 49
Set in a beautifully patterned marble surround, the gilt-brass altar front in the Sacred Heart Chapel depicts Judah pleading before Joseph for his brother Benjamin, and offering himself in his place (Genesis 44, vv. 33–34), an unusual choice of subject although its focus on redemptive sacrifice reflects the dedication of the chapel.

Fig. 50
The chancel. In the 1860s its walls were
lined with marble and alabaster, extending
the decorative scheme of the Sacred Heart
Chapel. At the same time, Henry Clutton,
architect of the chapel, designed the sedilia
(seats for the priests) on the right-hand side.
The matching arrangement opposite was
probably added by A. E. Purdie in the late
1880s; it originally supported a choir organ.

Clutton provided an additional touch of richness by piercing the wall between the chapel and the chancel with a three-bay arcade (see fig. 47) that projects on the chancel side to form a canopy for the sedilia (seats for the officiating clergy).

This splendid new chapel must have seemed to cast the rest of the church a little into the shade. While its builder, G. P. White, was at work on it, he was asked to undertake also the remodelling of the incomplete east aisle (which may have been damaged in the fire). Clutton rebuilt the three-bay arcade using red granite for the nave piers, and gave the aisle a rib vault in Caen stone, in place of Scoles's wooden lean-to roof. This was the point at which it would have been natural to have completed the aisle, but the land was still not available, and it was not until 1876 that the Jesuits were able to commission Clutton to finish the work begun nearly two decades earlier. The east aisle, opened in 1878, is a seamless continuation of his earlier work, but in an intriguing demonstration of the way that architectural tastes had shifted once more, back to English models of Gothic architecture, his proposal for the aisle windows – bold bar-tracery of thirteenth-century type – was rejected by the Jesuits in favour of fourteenth-century Decorated English forms, which were more in keeping with Scoles's church.[31]

Clutton referred to this change in 1883, two years after he had retired owing to failing sight, when he wrote to the Jesuits to remind them that they had still not paid him for his unexecuted drawings, among which were two sets of designs for a Sodality Chapel. The second, of 1878, was a revision, in Clutton's words, 'to suit the change in the epoch of the Architecture made from the original designs of the enlargement of the church'.[32] The Sodality of the Immaculate Conception, an association for laymen, had been founded in 1857 and was given the use of the Chapel of St Ignatius, to the west of the chancel. Clutton may be referring either to an intention to remodel or enlarge this chapel, or to construct a new chapel at the south end of the east aisle, but the work was not carried out.[33]

The outer east aisle is divided into three chapels, their altars set at right angles to the nave. At the southern end of this aisle is an enclosed space, which in 1905 became the Agony Chapel. On Clutton's plans, it appears as a porch, with an outer door opening onto Farm Street and an inner door leading into what became the Chapel of Our Lady of Lourdes. The space seems to have been left unfinished while the Jesuits debated linking this corner of the church to the residence for the Provincial that they planned to build next door in Farm Street.[34]

THE CHANCEL

The first major work at Farm Street to be carried out after the completion of the Sacred Heart Chapel was the remodelling of the chancel (fig. 50), which is undocumented. The walls were lined with alabaster and green Genoese marble – in effect, an extension of the decorative scheme of the Sacred Heart Chapel – and the floor level was raised. In his 1960 history of the

60

church, Fr Harold Roper gives a date of 1864 for this work, which he attributes to the architect Edward Goldie. Since Goldie was born in 1856, this must be an error for his father, George Goldie (1828–1887), who otherwise had no known connection with the church until 1883 (see below). If this is true, it is surprising that the job was not given to Clutton. Roper also states that on the orders of Fr Peter Gallwey, Rector since 1860, Goldie took the north window out and replaced it ten feet higher to lift it clear of the high altar.[35] The two large mosaics on the north wall, depicting the Annunciation and Coronation of Our Lady, were made by Salviati of Venice, the leading specialist in architectural mosaic, and installed in 1875 under Clutton's direction.[36]

As well as these major extensions and alterations to the church, there was a constant stream of small commissions for furnishings. In the early days almost all the functional fittings – confessionals, sacristy cupboards and so on – were made by a local firm of church furnishers, James Tayler of 3 Lower Seymour Street. Tayler was also responsible for a now-forgotten aspect of the church's architectural and decorative history, the elaborate temporary fittings erected for church festivals. For example, a detailed account survives for his work on the furnishings installed for the Feast of the Immaculate Conception in 1867:

> Preparing a very large set of sweeped [swept] Framings for the Altar window with cross rails, standards &c terminated with a Crown; taking to the Church, putting together and taking to pieces for Mr Crace to Decorate; afterwards fixing up complete over the window, fixing the Picture Drapery, Brass rods for candles, steps for flowers, Throne, Platform, Carpets &c &c after the Octave taking all down, clearing away, papering up and stowing away…[37]

Tayler charged fifteen guineas for the work, carried out in collaboration with J. G. Crace & Son, the eminent firm of interior decorators based in Wigmore Street, who had worked closely with Pugin.

GEORGE GOLDIE'S RISE AND FALL
The fitting out of the east chapels following the aisle's completion in 1878 was dependent on the generosity of individual donors. However, the artists and craftsmen involved were chosen by the architect, sometimes in collaboration with the clergy, and a consistent quality was achieved through the use of such leading firms as Rattee and Kett of Cambridge for carving and Samuel Ruddock of Lambeth for architectural sculpture.[38] The fittings of only two of these chapels – St Joseph (fig. 51) and St Francis Xavier (fig. 54) – were designed by Clutton. The other three, Our Lady of Lourdes (fig. 52), St Aloysius (fig. 53) and the Agony Chapel, are the work of the third architect to be extensively involved at Farm Street, Alfred Edward Purdie (1843–1920), who became the clergy's first choice partly as a result of an argument over Goldie's fitting out of the Chapel of Our Lady of Lourdes. Because of the dispute, the chapel is – uniquely for the eastern

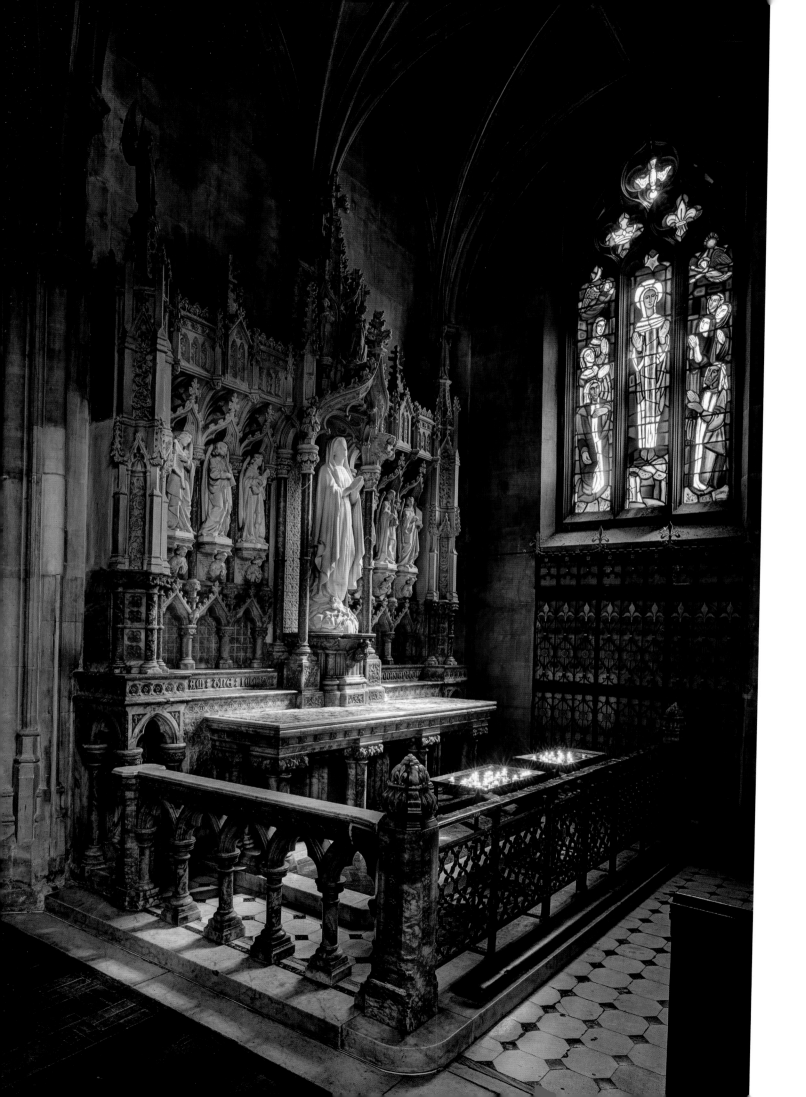

Fig. 52
The Chapel of Our Lady of
Lourdes. Its altarpiece was
designed by A. E. Purdie in
1885–86. The stained glass is
by Evie Hone (see also fig. 87).

Fig. 53
The Chapel of St Aloysius.
The altarpiece, designed by
A. E. Purdie, was carved by
London's leading firm of
architectural sculptors,
Farmer and Brindley.

chapels – well documented, and can form, therefore, a case study of the way each chapel was the result of a three-way collaboration between donor, clergy and designer.

In 1885 William Lyall, a recent convert – he had formerly been Rector of St Dionis Back-church in the City of London – offered money to fit out a new chapel at the south end of the inner east aisle, asking that it be dedicated to Our Lady of Lourdes. The commission was given to Goldie, Child and Goldie, probably on the recommendation of Fr Thomas Porter, Rector from 1881 to 1887. Established by George Goldie, who had taken his son, Edward (1856–1921), into partnership in 1880, the firm specialised in Gothic ecclesiastical work for Roman Catholic clients; their best-known work is the church of St James, Spanish Place, London, built in 1887–90. George Goldie's younger brother Charles (1835–1906) was an artist, who painted altarpieces for the St Joseph and St Francis Xavier chapels.[39] At the time George Goldie was given the commission for the Chapel of Our Lady of Lourdes, he was completing the residence at No. 31 Farm Street, immediately to the east of the church, for which contracts had been signed in February 1883.

This long-envisaged building, at last made possible when the site of the cottages adjacent to the church became available, included a residence for the Provincial, who was then based at Farm Street. Goldie's first design was published in *The Builder* in 1886 (fig. 55). It shows an attractively picturesque stone-faced building of three gabled storeys stepping down at the east to a single storey, so matching the scale of the surrounding humble mews houses and stables. Goldie explained that 'The desire of the architects was to work up to and embody the style of the church and the beautiful side porch as far as possible'. He proposed incorporating Clutton's porch at the south end of the outer east aisle into his new building, to double as a porch to the church and an entrance hall to the residence. However, the Jesuits decided against this idea, and asked Goldie to redesign the building, as he explained in *The Builder* – clearly with regret:

*Subsequently, other plans were made and realised, with a separate side porch or vestibule,
so curtailing the interior accommodation on the ground-floor, as the site at disposal was
very limited indeed. These changes, together with the necessity of meeting further special
requirements, have added considerably to the height of the building, which has an elevation in brick, very nearly as plain and flat as it could be designed.*

This fairly describes the bulky four-storey block (with basement and attic) that was completed
in 1885, its façade on Farm Street relieved only by Gothic detail around the main door and blind
arches at the attic stage (fig. 56).[40] As well as accommodation for the Provincial, it included
reading rooms, a refectory and (on the top floor) a library.

Only a few months after the building was completed, Goldie found himself out of favour.
When Lyall saw the completed altar of Our Lady of Lourdes in January 1886 he was disap-
pointed. He had asked that the statue of Our Lady be a replica of the one in the grotto at Lourdes,
and had envisaged therefore a freestanding figure. However, Goldie and the sculptor, Alexandre
Chertier of Paris, had reproduced the Lourdes statue in high relief. In reply to Porter, who had
communicated Lyall's displeasure, Goldie wrote back, somewhat nettled, pointing out that both
Porter and Lyall had been shown not only a drawing but also a model of the proposed altar and
had raised no objection to his design.[41] Lyall was adamant that since he had wanted a statue
one would have to be provided, and so Goldie reluctantly sought an estimate for a replacement from Thomas Earp. However, Porter lost patience with him, and took the commission
away: 'I rejoice to hear that Mr Goldie is to be got rid of,' wrote Lyall uncharitably in July 1886.[42]
Goldie's altar was banished to the Cathedral of the Immaculate Conception in Guyana, which
was staffed by the Jesuits (and incidentally had a tower by Ignatius Scoles), where it was lost in
the fire that destroyed the building in 1913.

Probably in consequence, this was the end of Goldie's involvement at Farm Street and
the chapel was handed instead to Purdie, then busy with the new presbytery in Mount Street
(see below). When the leading firm of architectural sculptors in London, Farmer and Brindley
– who had provided the sculpture for Purdie's altar of St Aloysius – proved too expensive (at
£750), Purdie gave the commission for the statue of Our Lady of Lourdes to the obscure sculptor
Frederick Anstey of New Cross, south London, for £500. However, Anstey provided only a model
for the figure, which was carved in marble at Carrara (fig. 57) and paid for by a friend of Porter,
Thomas Pate, a merchant in Livorno. This episode reveals clearly that although the choice of
architect for fitting out a chapel was usually the clergy's, and the craftsmen were selected by the
architect, the final word in a design was the donor's.

Fig. 57
The reredos in the Chapel of Our Lady of Lourdes. The altarpiece replaced one by George Goldie that displeased the donor, William Lyall, as the Virgin Mary was depicted in high relief, and not as a free-standing sculpture like that in the grotto at Lourdes on which the figure is based. Purdie's figure was carved in Carrara, Italy, from a model by a London sculptor, Frederick Anstey.

A. E. PURDIE

Although now largely forgotten, Purdie had a substantial practice in the last quarter of the nineteenth century, specialising in handsome but old-fashioned Gothic churches for Roman Catholic clients, such as his two most prominent London buildings, Our Lady Help of Christians at Blackheath (1890–91) and the English Martyrs at Streatham (1892–97). The clergy at Farm Street were loyal clients, and the letters from him that survive in their archive – more numerous than those from any other architect – give an impression of affable efficiency.

Purdie's major work for the Jesuits is the large presbytery on Mount Street, on land owned by the Duke of Westminster's Grosvenor Estate (fig. 58). In 1868 the Jesuits had taken a lease of 111 Mount Street, and shortly afterwards added No. 112. In 1872 they asked Clutton to design a presbytery and elementary school on the site of these houses, a job that he passed to his former pupil J. F. Bentley. Bentley prepared drawings for the scheme, but the proposal was rejected by the Grosvenor Estate, because it was beginning to make plans for the comprehensive redevelopment of Mount Street.[43] By the mid-1880s the character of this part of Mayfair was rapidly moving up in the world, helped by the demolition of the St George's parish workhouse in 1885 and the decision that its site (together with the adjoining cemetery) would be laid out as public gardens rather than redeveloped. Having decided to demolish Nos 111 and 112 Mount Street, the Jesuits collaborated with the Grosvenor Estate on Purdie's design for their replacement (to be renumbered No. 114 Mount Street), in the style – Franco-Flemish 'Queen Anne' – and materials – pink brick and terracotta – specified by the estate. The building, which is linked to the sacristies at the north-east corner of the church, and incorporates a Sodality Hall and Chapel (fig. 59), was completed in 1887 at a cost of £16,000. The estate's decision to leave a gap between Nos 114 and 113 provided not only public access from Mount Street to the new gardens, but also for the first time a clear view of the north front of the church. Purdie inserted a door into the gardens from the Chapel of St Ignatius, as part of his remodelling of the chapel with a new altar on a spectacular scale, costing £1,350 and completed in 1888.[44] His final work in the church was to fit out the Agony Chapel in 1905, by when he had virtually retired from practice. This was almost the last addition to the church, since two years earlier the west aisle had at last been completed by an architect possessing a fertility of invention that Purdie never attempted to emulate.[45]

THE WEST AISLE

In April 1891 the Rector, Fr James Hayes, printed a notice announcing that the Jesuits had acquired the freehold of the Immaculate Conception from the Berkeley Estate the month before for £23,000, a sum that included the purchase of 'the piece of land which ultimately will be needed for the completion of the church'.[46] A design for the new aisle was not sought until 1898, almost certainly to allow for fundraising, but even so the chosen architect, W. H. Romaine-

Figs 58, 59
The presbytery in Mount Street, north-
east of the church, designed by A. E. Purdie
in the 'Queen Anne' style specified by the
Grosvenor Estate, on whose land it stands.
Completed in 1887, it includes a hall and
chapel (*right*, in a Victorian photograph by
Mayall & Co., 126 Piccadilly) for the church's
association for laymen, the Sodality of the
Immaculate Conception.

Walker (1854–1940), was not impressed by the budget he was offered: 'the sum you mention
(£10,000)', he wrote, 'would be in my estimation ample to build a North Aisle & Chapels but
not to erect it as I had wished to, namely, equal to, if not superior in every detail to the work of
the South aisle & chapels'.[47] He proposed £20,000, and although the Jesuits protested that they
could have built a whole church for that sum, we must be grateful that Romaine-Walker got
his way, as the aisle is both his ecclesiastical masterpiece and a magnificent climax to the architectural history of the church. In the letter accompanying his design, Romaine-Walker wrote:
'I would conclude by saying my only object is to do the very best for the church & I should wish
you to understand that the word trouble does not exist so far as I am personally concerned.'[48]

Fig. 60
The Chapel of St Ignatius. The enormous
altarpiece, the largest at Farm Street, was
designed by A. E. Purdie for the previous
chapel on this site and completed in 1888.
Ten years later it was moved into the new
chapel designed by W. H. Romaine-Walker
as part of his remodelling of the north-
west corner of the church. The sculpture
on the left, by Charles Whiffen, depicts
St Francis Xavier holding a crucifix aloft
(see also fig. 62) – perhaps the one he
lost overboard on one of his missionary
voyages that was miraculously returned
to him by a crab.

The archive offers no clue as to why he was chosen for the job. He was the first architect to work on the church who was not a Roman Catholic, and his fashionable, aristocratic practice was associated more with houses. While busy at Farm Street he was collaborating with the architect and garden designer Achille Duchêne on the design of Sunderland House, the Duke of Marlborough's huge mansion in Curzon Street (1899–1901), and he was employed by the Duke of Devonshire for alterations at Chatsworth and by the Earl of Derby for extensions to Knowsley. Nonetheless, he had a good pedigree as a Gothic designer, having been a pupil of George Edmund Street, architect of the Royal Courts of Justice, and in 1899 he designed one of the last great Gothic houses, Stanhope House in Park Lane, for the soap magnate R. W. Hudson.

Romaine-Walker's extension is a double aisle, as intended by Scoles, of which the inner one, for seating, is a close copy of Clutton's on the east. The outer aisle – which replaced the three bays that Scoles had been able to build – incorporates four chapels facing into the church, and the octagonal Calvary Chapel at the south-west corner. Since the Jesuits wanted to provide a more formal entrance to the church at the north, Scoles's St Ignatius Chapel was demolished and replaced by a larger, clerestoried chapel (fig. 60) separated from the chancel by a passage leading to a north porch. Purdie's fittings, completed only ten years before, were moved into this new chapel.[49]

The land acquired for the new aisle was insufficiently wide for external buttresses, prompting Romaine-Walker to a brilliantly inventive idea. The outer aisle is supported by internal buttresses, which enclose top-lit confessionals on a triangular plan, alternating with the chapels, which are therefore polygonal (on the model, according to Romaine-Walker, of the eastern chapels at Westminster Abbey). The entrance to the confessionals is concealed from the body of the church by piers on which statues of saints are mounted. The alternating piers rise on axis with the chapel's altars, partly screening them, a point for which Romaine-Walker has been criticised, although the aisle gains thereby a powerful element of spatial complexity (fig. 63 and pages 6–7).

This ingenuity in planning is equalled by inventiveness in the decorative detail. At dado level the aisle is animated by a blind arcade of projecting ogee arches, a mid-fourteenth-century English motif (seen most famously in the Lady Chapel at Ely Cathedral) that is known to architectural historians as a 'nodding ogee', a term that captures its strong element of movement. The dado is capped by an openwork stone frieze of French Flamboyant character, producing a mixture of Gothic idioms that echoes Scoles's south front. A final inventive touch is the lighting of the Calvary Chapel by means of a glass dome above open tracery (see pages 4–5), an idea that may have been derived from the Chapel of the Constable of Castile at Burgos Cathedral.

The quality of the aisle's architecture is matched by its fittings (including the altar rails, unfortunately removed in the 1970s).[50] These were expensive: for example, Romaine-Walker's estimate for the Altar of the Seven Dolours (fig. 66) was £1,187, which drew a protest from the

74

Fig. 61
The Calvary in the Chapel
of St Ignatius, designed
by W. H. Romaine-Walker
and carved by the Belgian
sculptor Alphonse de
Wispelaere. The donor,
Baroness von Bissing,
specified that the figures
be of white marble, but
Romaine-Walker was able
to introduce some colour
in the cross by his choice
of a bluish marble, the long
veins of which, he wrote,
'suggest the texture of wood'.

Rector.[51] When Romaine-Walker died in 1940, his obituarist in *The Builder* commented that he was an exacting critic of the craftsmen he employed, but 'those who worked with and under him felt that the final results were often immeasurably the better for the additional labour involved'.[52] This may help to explain why the statues outside the confessionals are masterpieces, despite the fact that their sculptor was – and remains – an obscure figure. Charles Whiffen (*c.* 1868–1929) was a young sculptor and medallist living in Cheltenham when Romaine-Walker offered him the commission.[53] Apart from his work at Farm Street he is now remembered only for his monumental sculpture on the Victory Arch that forms the principal pedestrian entrance to Waterloo Station, completed in 1922 as a war memorial for the London and South Western Railway. It was almost certainly Romaine-Walker's idea that Whiffen's Farm Street sculptures should be made of coloured marbles. There was a Europe-wide fashion in the 1890s for polychromatic sculpture by such avant-garde artists as Max Klinger or Jean-Léon Gérôme, but whereas most examples employed mixed media – marble with ivory or bronze, for example – Whiffen executed each sculpture with great virtuosity almost exclusively in marble (fig. 62). The most admired figure is St Margaret of Scotland (fig. 68), whose garments alone incorporate Irish red, Welsh green and Canadian blue marbles; the only parts not of marble are her buttons, of mother-of-pearl, and the cross she holds, made of Irish bog oak.[54]

Romaine-Walker did not seek equivalent originality in the paintings that form altarpieces in the west aisle. He chose instead copies of Old Master paintings, most strikingly in the Calvary Chapel (fig. 64), where the triptych over the altar is a copy of part of a late fifteenth-century fresco by Pietro Perugino, *The Crucifixion and Saints*, in the church of Santa Maria Maddalena dei Pazzi in Florence. All these paintings are by a talented copyist, the Neapolitan-born Julia Gambardella (1851–1931), who lived in Islington. In 1904 Romaine-Walker dismissed a suggestion from the Jesuits that he might commission a painting for one of the altarpieces from the artist Albert Chevallier Tayler (1862–1925), who was then working on a cycle of paintings depicting the Life of St Ignatius for the Church of the Sacred Heart at Wimbledon: 'I know Mr Chevalier Taylor [*sic*] very well – also his work. I had only allowed the cost of copies of Old Masters in the Reredos & frankly I think they wd be much better. However shd you wish me to ask Mr Taylor I will do so tho' the cost will, of necessity, be a good deal more.'[55] As well as keeping costs down, Romaine-Walker doubtless wanted to use an artist who would be completely under his control, as Chevallier Taylor would almost certainly not have been.

THE CHURCH IN THE TWENTIETH CENTURY

If Romaine-Walker had had his way, the west aisle would not have formed the final climax to the building. He proposed a rebuilding of all the upper parts of the church, to the same height but with a three-storey, cathedral-like elevation, incorporating a triforium as well as a

Fig. 62
Charles Whiffen's polychrome statue of St Francis Xavier in the Chapel of St Ignatius.

Fig. 63
This view of the west aisle, showing the Chapel of Our Lady and St Stanislaus, captures the spatial and decorative complexity of W. H. Romaine-Walker's addition to the church. On the left is a statue by Charles Whiffen of St Winefrid, martyred because she refused to marry a pagan prince. The statue on the right, which depicts St Frances of Rome and her son, was carved by Joseph Swynnerton.

Fig. 64 (overleaf)
The Calvary Chapel. The altarpiece was painted by Julia Gambardella and the sculpture is by Joseph Swynnerton – on the left *The Man of Sorrows* (loosely derived from an engraving by Albrecht Dürer) and on the right the *Mater Dolorosa*. Romaine-Walker's lighting of the chapel is achieved by means of a glass dome above open tracery (see pages 4–5), which may have been derived from the Chapel of the Constable of Castile at Burgos Cathedral.

Fig. 65
The reredos in the Calvary Chapel,
a copy of part of a late fifteenth-
century fresco by Perugino,
The Crucifixion and Saints, in
Santa Maria Maddalena dei Pazzi
in Florence.

Fig. 66
The Chapel of Seven Dolours.
In the altarpiece the sculpture of
the Virgin, by Charles Whiffen, is
flanked by panels of saints
painted by Julia Gambardella
after Mantegna and Verrocchio.

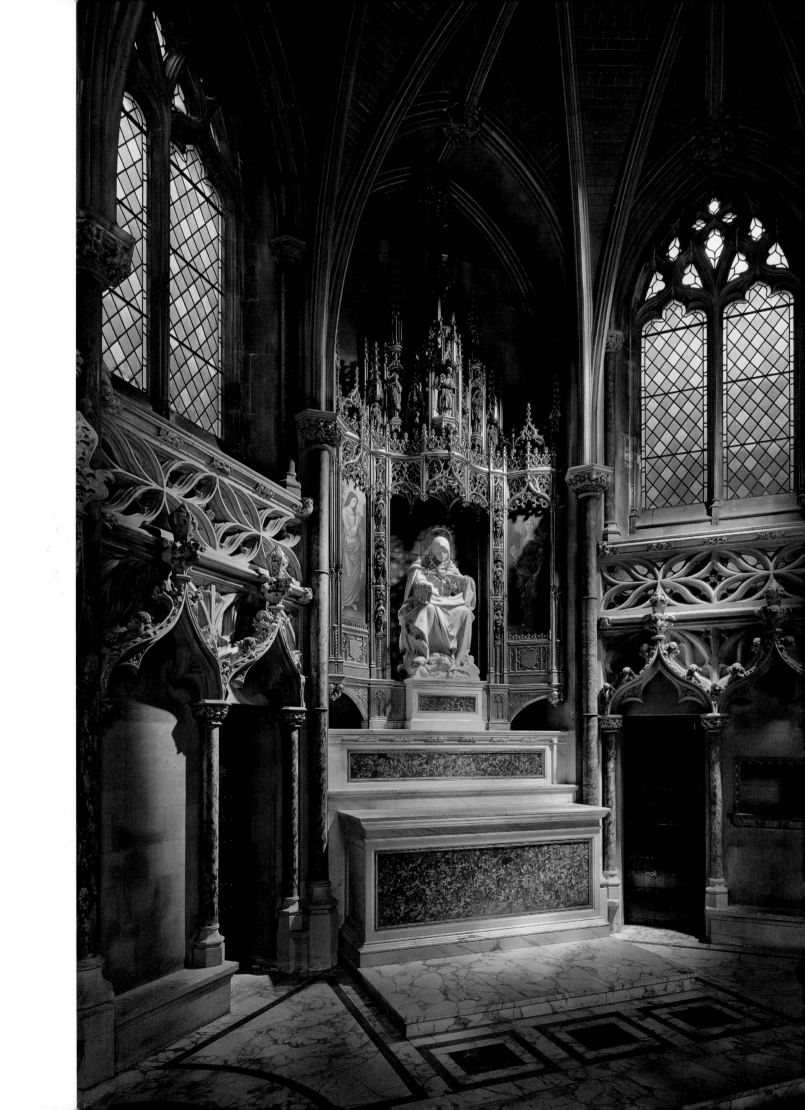

Figs 67, 68
St Ignatius (*left*) and
St Margaret of Scotland (*right*),
two of the polychromatic
marble sculptures by
Charles Whiffen that are the
outstanding artistic treasures
of the church. St Ignatius is
depicted preaching, standing
on a plinth inlaid with green
malachite. Whiffen's handling
of his materials in the statue
of St Margaret is a tour-de-force:
her inner garment is of red
Irish marble banded with
green marble from Caernarfon;
the blue marble of her cloak
came from Canada.

84

Figs 69, 70
The Chapel of St Stanislaus. W. H. Romaine-
Walker incorporated into the altarpiece
what may well be the earliest sculpture in
the church. This anonymous carving of the
Annunciation was made for the Chapel of
St Ignatius, from which it was displaced
in the 1880s by Purdie's vast new altar
(see fig. 60). The recumbent statue of the
Jesuit St Stanislaus Kostka (1550–1568)
(*below*) is a monochrome copy of one
by Pierre Legros, carved in 1702–03 for
Sant'Andrea al Quirinale in Rome.

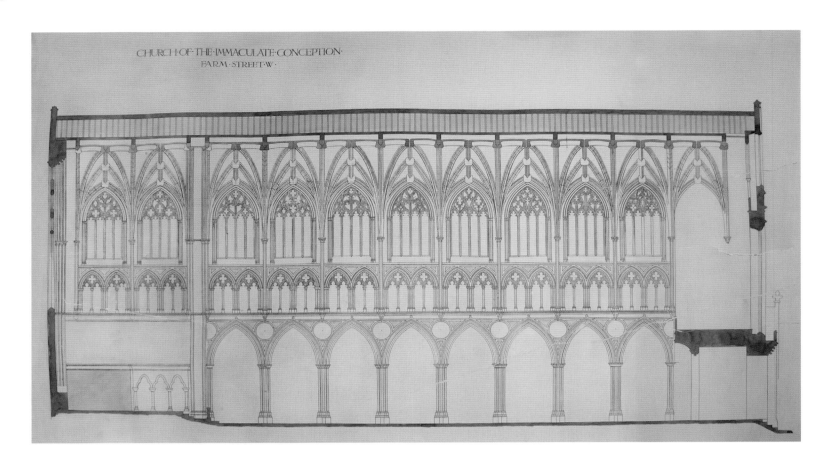

CHURCH·OF·THE·IMMACULATE·CONCEPTION·
FARM·STREET·W·

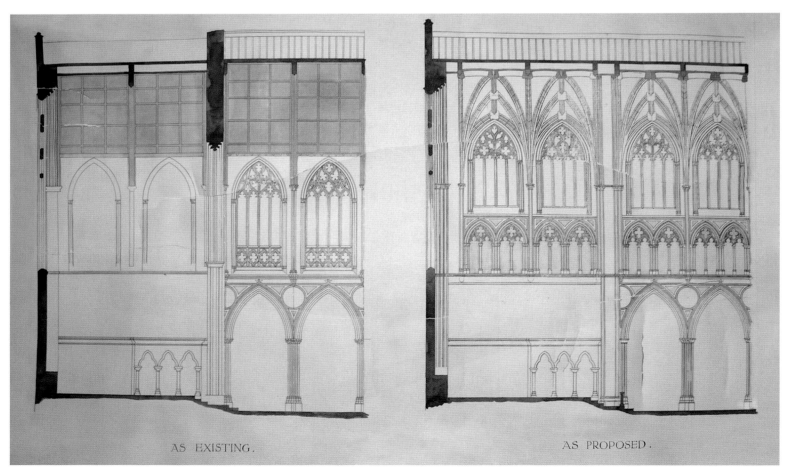

AS EXISTING.   AS PROPOSED.

Figs 71.1–2
These undated drawings by W. H. Romaine-
Walker show his extravagant and unexecuted
proposal for rebuilding the upper parts of the
church with a taller clerestory and a rib vault.

clerestory, rising to a stone rib vault. Since he prepared a full set of (undated) design drawings for these changes (figs 71.1–2), together with a lost perspective to illustrate what he intended, there must have been serious discussion about this extravagantly expensive proposal, although nothing came of it.[56] However, the luxuriant splendour of Romaine-Walker's work – which included a new chancel rail, designed in 1901 and made of marble inset with lapis lazuli (figs 44 and 72) – must have caused the clergy to look with a more critical eye on the church's existing furnishings.[57] Dissatisfied with the dirty condition of Wailes's north window, in 1912 they commissioned Hardman of Birmingham to replace it.[58]

Since its stained glass was removed for safekeeping at the onset of the Second World War, Hardman's new north window survived the severe damage inflicted on the church during the Blitz. In an air raid on the night of 22 September 1940 incendiary bombs ignited the roof, destroying almost a third of it (fig. 82). The church was closed and services were continued in the chapel in the Mount Street building. Then, on the night of 16–17 April 1941, during intensive bombing, a high explosive landed in Farm Street, badly damaging the south front of the church and shattering its remaining glass. Repairs, supervised by the architect Adrian Gilbert Scott (1882–1963), were not completed until 1951 (fig. 40). In 1953 stained glass by the Irish artist Evie Hone (1894–1955), depicting the Instruments of the Passion, was installed in the south front's rose window (fig. 89). Hone also supplied glass for the lancets above the rose and for the three-light window (representing the Assumption of the Blessed Virgin) in the Lourdes Chapel (fig. 87). Further work intended by Hone was forestalled by her death, but in 1964 Patrick Pollen, who had inherited her studio, provided a window (depicting English martyrs) for the south end of the west aisle (fig. 88).

As a result of liturgical changes imposed following the Second Vatican Council of 1963–65, the chancel was reordered to allow the celebrant to face the congregation during Mass. In 1980 the architects Broadbent, Hastings, Reid & New extended the chancel floor to accommodate a forward altar, and moved the pulpit northwards to the chancel arch. However, the chancel did not take its present form until 1992, following debate about how to accommodate Pugin's high altar to the new liturgical requirements. The solution finally adopted was to leave the altar in its original location, and make a fibreglass cast of its lower part for use as the forward altar.

Discovery in 1987 of dry rot in two of the main trusses in the nave roof led to major remedial works under the direction of the architect Austin Winkley; as part of this work the ceiling was decorated with a stencilled pattern designed by Mr Winkley (fig. 43), replacing a scheme painted as part of the post-war repairs.[59] What must surely be the final major decorative addition to the church are the fourteen mosaic roundels in the spandrels of the nave arcades. Made in 1996 by Filomena Monteiro working with a member of the church's clergy, Fr Michael Beattie, they spell out the 'Ave Maria', illustrated with motifs inspired by the Salviati mosaics on the north wall of the church.[60]

Fig. 72 (overleaf)
The original gilt-bronze gates for
W. H. Romaine-Walker's chancel rail
(see fig. 44). They are now in
the Calvary Chapel.

Figs 73, 74
The north window (*right*)
and a detail of its spectacular
tracery (*left*), which J. J. Scoles
based on the east window of
Carlisle Cathedral. By 1912
its original glass, by William
Wailes, had become so dirty
that it was replaced by a new
window, depicting the Tree
of Jesse, made by Hardman
of Birmingham. The window
was taken into storage during
the Second World War, and
so survived the bombs that
destroyed almost all the rest
of the church's glass.

MATERABILIS   RO·N·

MARIA PERRY

FARM STREET BETWEEN THE WARS AND BEYOND

By the first decades of the twentieth century the Church of the Immaculate Conception at Farm Street was established as one of the most fashionable places of worship in London. This was due not only to the excellence of its clergy, the brilliance of their sermons and their reputation for soundness of doctrine, but also to its Mayfair location, which gave it an advantage over London's other Catholic churches. When the Oratory, with its mighty dome and 240-foot nave, was being planned, Cardinal Newman had been perturbed by the faint aura of shabbiness that clung to Brompton in those days: 'That suburb,' he objected, 'that neighbourhood of second-rate gentry and second-rate shops.'[1] No such stigma was attached to Mayfair. Visiting dignitaries and foreign royalty were frequently drawn to Farm Street, simply because of its proximity to where they happened to be staying.

In November 1913 the Queen of Spain and the former Empress Eugénie attended a Requiem Mass for Mme d'Arcos at Farm Street (fig. 30), and in the same month the Archduke Franz Ferdinand of Austria and his wife, Duchess Sophie of Hohenburg, arrived in London. They attended Mass at Farm Street regularly throughout their visit. Six months later their assassination in Sarajevo on 28 June 1914 was to provoke the outbreak of the First World War. The casualties of what was later dubbed 'the war that came out of the air' were so appalling that by September 1914 Masses were being offered every Friday at Farm Street for all Catholics in the British Forces who had given their lives for their country.

Although Fr Charles Nicholson was Superior, Fr Bernard Vaughan (fig. 76) was by far the most popular priest. Vaughan had spent many years at the Church of the Holy Name in Manchester, but he created a great stir at Farm Street, where in 1906, in the middle of the London Season, he preached an exceptionally popular series of sermons on 'The Sins of Society'. With hindsight, this seems an unlikely topic to have inspired Mayfair. Eight years later, at the outbreak of war, his rousing, patriotic sermons, such as 'England! Behold the Man!', attracted immediate attention.

By the end of 1914 Fr Terence Donnelly, for twelve years Rector of Stamford Hill, had become the new Superior. He remained throughout the war. Donnelly had built both the church and the college at Stamford Hill, but Vaughan's influence at Farm Street went far beyond the confines of the church buildings. His book *What of Today* went into five editions. In 1915 he preached sermons entitled 'Where Are Our Brave Dead Gone?' and 'Where Are You Going after Death?' By then the Blitz was under way. In the earliest months of the war Londoners feared that the Germans might send Zeppelins, their notorious airships that had already bombed Belgium with deadly effect, but Kaiser Wilhelm II had forbidden such attacks on London out of concern for the British royal family, to whom he was related. It was not until January 1915 that he sanctioned the bombing of England. As the war progressed, London was hit many times. It was among the stricken and the bereaved that Vaughan brought his message of hope and

Fig. 75
A ceramic sculpture of the Madonna and Child in the Chapel of the English Martyrs, in the style of the Italian Renaissance Della Robbia workshop. Its plinth was designed and carved by Eric Gill in 1925.

resurrection. In 1916 he repeated 'England! Behold the Man!' In the same year the Daughters of the Heart of Mary began managing St Joseph's Library, then in South Audley Street and later at 22 Farm Street. Although the premises had been converted from some stables, the Sisters' care and devotion created a little haven of normality in the war-torn capital.

Vaughan's golden jubilee as a priest took place that December, and Pope Benedict XV sent him a portable altar as a gift, which he used in his work in the East End, where the air raids were at their worst. The cruellest attack came on 13 June 1917, when a group of Gothas, the aircraft that superseded the Zeppelins, destroyed Upper North Street Primary School in East London in broad daylight. Fifteen children were killed and many more injured. Parents searched frantically for children as young as five, trapped under the rubble. Ambulances carried tiny infants, some dying, most screaming, to local hospitals.

In March 1917 the illustrious musician Guy Weitz, a pupil of Widor, became Organist at Farm Street. He was also a composer and an Honorary Organist at Westminster Cathedral. Many of his stirring voluntaries were first performed at Farm Street. After forty years' service, in 1957, he was awarded the Pro Ecclesia et Pontifice medal, but his first duty was to play at requiems for the war dead. In February 1919, only three months after the Armistice, a Solemn Requiem was held for those old boys of Stonyhurst who had died in battle. Fr Vaughan preached and Fr Bede Jarrett, the Dominican Provincial, attended. Fr Vaughan's fame had spread so widely throughout London during the First World War bombing that grateful East End workers and their children presented him with his portrait in oils, which was hung at Stonyhurst. Later, a wax model of him was exhibited at Madame Tussaud's. In October Fr Arthur Day, who had been a War Chaplain, arrived at Farm Street. He worked tirelessly among London's Jewish community, was frequently to be seen preaching at Hyde Park Corner and in 1922 joined the Catholic Guild of Israel. In December Fr Charles Galton became Superior. Having held the post with distinction throughout the war, Fr Donnelly retired to the Jesuit Community of the Sacred Heart at Wimbledon.

Fr Galton introduced weekly Pulpit Dialogues, which saw two speakers expressing different viewpoints on the same subject from pulpits on opposite sides of the church; these ran throughout the summer months of 1920 and proved immensely popular. As bombed sites were cleared and London started to recover, a series of energetic preachers visited Farm Street to expound on the theme of thanksgiving. Among them was the newly ordained Fr Ronald Knox, who made a dashing debut on the Feast of St Ignatius. By that time the apotheosis of Fr Vaughan, whose waxwork had become a permanent installation at Madame Tussaud's,

Fig. 76
Fr Bernard Vaughan and his brother with their car, which they had transformed into a mobile chapel so that they could drive all over the country to hold services. Photograph *Süddeutsche Zeitung*. Mary Evans Picture Library

added greatly to the prestige of the Farm Street Community. In December, *The Tablet* published an article describing the Christmas Crib:

> *An impressive representation of the story of Bethlehem is seen this year at Farm Street, so life-like are the figures, so realistic the effect. Two distinguished artists have been responsible for this striking reproduction of cinque cento Italian art, Mr Percy McQuoid, who designed it, and Mr Phil Harker, who has carried out the work with wonderful perfection of detail and illusion. As one stands in the outer darkness of the church and gazes through the slender arches at this picture, it might be that a masterpiece of Botticelli had come to life, so perfect is its crystal purity of atmosphere and blue distances.*[2]

Throughout the next two years the Pulpit Dialogues continued, and St Ignatius was declared Patron of the Spiritual Exercises. According to Fr Cyril Martindale (fig. 35), one of the best-known writers of the time, Fr Vaughan continued to 'wear himself out in God's service, preaching, lecturing and giving retreats'.[3] In addition to his ordinary priestly activities he had been Director of the Sodality of the Immaculate Conception for twenty years. He was sent to South Africa for a rest cure, but resting was not in his nature. He returned to Mount Street exhausted and died there on 31 October 1922. The news was announced all over London, and rich and poor of all denominations thronged to his requiem. He was buried at Kensal Green.

The Pulpit Dialogues were eventually replaced by a series of lectures in the Sodality Hall. Every Catholic was expected to bring a non-Catholic visitor. The speakers included G. K. Chesterton, Hilaire Belloc, Fr Bede Jarrett and other luminaries. By 1924 the Catholic Students' Society had also begun to meet regularly at 114 Mount Street. In the six years since the Armistice and amid the hedonism of the Roaring Twenties, the seeds of Farm Street's Outreach Programme had been sown, and they had blossomed beyond all expectation. Several priests who were eminent writers also joined the Farm Street Community at this time. Fr Leo Hicks, an expert on Tudor history, arrived in 1924, followed in 1925 by Fr James Brodrick, a broadcaster who was also the biographer of St Ignatius Loyola and St Francis Xavier.[4] Fortuitously Brodrick decided to write about the Blessed Peter Canisius, who was canonised in May 1925 and declared a Doctor of the Church. In January 1926 Fr Galton left Farm Street for Stamford Hill to be succeeded as Superior by Fr Robert Steuart, another gifted writer. An army chaplain during the war, he was subsequently Superior of St Aloysius, the Jesuit church in Oxford. While at Farm Street Steuart published several notable works of spiritual guidance, among them *The Inward Vision, Temples of Eternity, World Intangible* and, in 1936, *The Divinity of Holiness*. These books were read by Catholics and non-Catholics alike, and gained their author some distinguished admirers, including William Inge, the Anglican Professor of Divinity at Cambridge, later Dean of St Paul's, and Mahatma Gandhi, who went to Farm Street on 25 November 1931 expressly to hear Steuart preach.

By 1926 the organ – installed in 1889 – was in need of repairs; it was renovated and modernised just in time for Christmas at a cost of £1,800. Guy Weitz gave a series of successful recitals to cover the expense. Shortly afterwards Fr John Driscoll, who had trained the choir at Wimbledon, took on the Farm Street choir as well. He brought Fernand Laloux with him from Wimbledon. Laloux and Weitz soon made Farm Street's musical reputation invincible. Laloux was to remain as Choirmaster at Farm Street until 1964. Fr Driscoll continued to advise, but as there was no school attached to Farm Street, he had great difficulty finding boys whose voices had not broken. Nevertheless, the respected music critic Ernest Newman described the 'perfect singing of the Farm Street choir' and thought it 'one of the finest choirs in the country'.[5] The quality of the sermons kept pace. In 1927, on the Feast of the Immaculate Conception, Fr Martin D'Arcy came from Oxford to preach. Cardinal Francis Bourne attended and the church was full to overflowing. Fr D'Arcy (fig. 77), England's leading Catholic intellectual, was a brilliant theologian who made many converts. A popular rhyme, mischievously celebrating his activities among the *jeunesse dorée* of Oxford and London, ran thus:

> *Are you rich and nobly born?*
> *Is your Soul by troubles torn?*
> *Come, and I shall heal them all.*
> *Martin D'Arcy, Campion Hall.*

Throughout the 1930s Fr D'Arcy gave Catholic instruction to a series of distinguished converts. Evelyn Waugh (fig. 78), who sought consolation after his brief marriage to Evelyn Gardner had broken down, was perhaps to become the most famous. A disconsolate, hard-drinking journalist, he had left Oxford with a third, but published a popular novel, *Decline and Fall*, in 1928 about his experiences as a schoolmaster in Wales. He lunched on 7 July 1930 with Noël Coward at the Ritz and mentioned his intention of embracing Catholicism. Coward advised him to give up the idea and travel: 'Go round the world.'[6] Waugh did not take this advice. The following day his diary records: 'Went to Father D'Arcy at 11. Blue chin and fine, slippery mind. The clergyhouse at Mount Street superbly ill-furnished. Anglicans can never achieve this ruthless absence of "good taste". We talked about verbal inspiration and Noah's Ark.'[7] On 29 September 1930 Waugh was received into the Roman Catholic church by Fr D'Arcy. His career had prospered that year with the publication of *Vile Bodies*, the enduring novel that captures so vividly the restless spirit of Mayfair between the wars. Less well known is his biography of Edmund Campion, which won the Hawthornden Prize in 1936.

Fig. 77
Fr Martin D'Arcy, *c.* 1931–32.
Photograph by Herbert Vandyke

Winds of change swept Farm Street in the 1930s. The most practical innovation was the installation of a passenger lift at 114 Mount Street, to the delight of all residents. Another surprise was that in 1931 Cardinal Bourne asked Fr Francis Devas, who came to Farm Street in 1920 and remained until his death in 1951, to be the ecclesiastical adviser to the Actors' Interval Club; this was the beginning of a long association between Farm Street and the English stage. The Farm Street choir made recordings for Columbia in November 1931, and these were used the following year at the Dublin Eucharistic Congress. In 1932 the exterior of the church was cleaned, bringing its fine stonework into glorious relief amid the red-brick surroundings. In 1933 the Beatification of Fr Joseph Pignatelli was celebrated. The Abbot of Buckfast preached on the Feast of St Ignatius, and in November a series of Dialogues was arranged by Fr Devas and Fr Francis Woodlock, comparing St Ignatius's *Spiritual Exercises* with the 'Spiritual Technique' of the Anglicans, as developed by the Oxford Group. These caused much intellectual controversy and drew large audiences. The church was also the focus of considerable excitement in February 1934, when the Jesuit Martyrs of South America were beatified, as in November were the Martyrs of Paraguay. Fr D'Arcy, by this time Master of Campion Hall in Oxford, came to Farm Street to preach on the Feast of the Immaculate Conception; he had lost none of his charisma. Fr Steuart left in 1935 for Wimbledon and was succeeded by Fr George Gallagher, who had been twice Vice-Provincial of the Jesuit Order. One event dominated that year, however: the Canonisation of the two indigenous saints, John Fisher and Sir Thomas More (fig. 79), whose relics were brought to Farm Street for veneration.

Following *Quadragesima Anno*, the papal encyclical of 1931, four conferences entitled 'The Catholic Church and Social Reform' were held at Farm Street during 1936. Two years later a most beautiful gift of a statue of St Thérèse of Lisieux (fig. 80) was received by Fr Gallagher. Known popularly as 'the Little Flower', she is sculpted in cream and brown marble to represent her habit as a Carmelite nun and holds a plain wooden cross as a symbol of her suffering. Two years were to pass before the statue was erected. By then it bore a plaque, explaining in Latin that it was the gift of 'clients, who devoutly cherish her spirit and virtues in the year of salvation 1940'.[8] The delay had been caused by uncertainty over where to place the Carmelite saint, who is traditionally venerated for her attention to 'little things'. When it was remembered that she is also a Patron of the Missions, she was positioned opposite the Calvary Chapel. Photographs of the saint appear on the wall beside the statue.

During the 1938 opera season at Covent Garden the Italian tenor Beniamino Gigli advertised for a boy to sing solo in *Tosca*. From the five hundred hopeful applicants, the boy soloist was chosen from the Farm Street choir. *Tosca* was broadcast and the performance was reviewed

Fig. 78
Evelyn Waugh in his major's uniform, *c.* 1940. Photographer unknown. Hulton Archive Collection

Figs 79, 80 (overleaf)
The Chapel of the English Martyrs (*left*). Charles Whiffen's statue portrays St Thomas More, whose hand rests on his executioner's axe. He is flanked by painted panels depicting English martyrs. The altar front is a single slab of jasper. The statue of St Thérèse of Lisieux (*right*), at the southern end of the west aisle, depicts her wearing the habit of a Carmelite sister, delicately carved in cream and brown marbles.

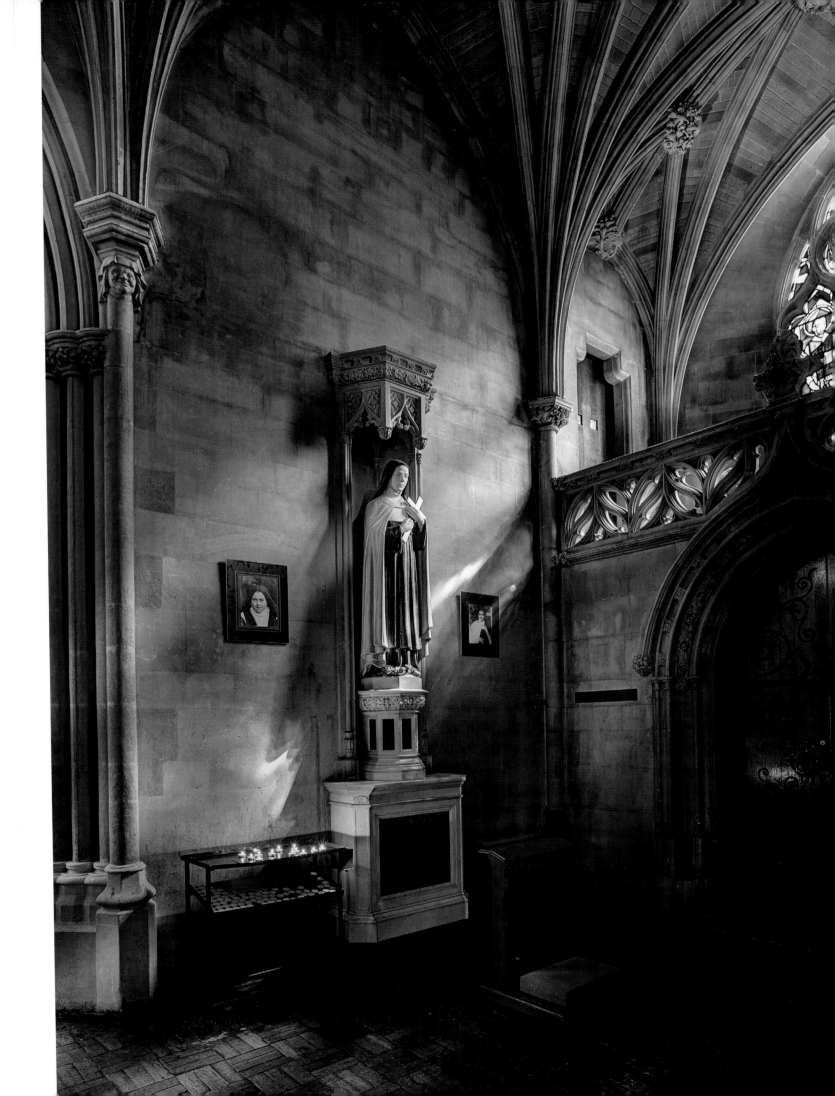

in all the London papers, bringing flattering publicity for the Farm Street choir. In December of that year Fr Gallagher was succeeded by Fr Leonard Geddes as Superior. A professor of theology, he had taught for many years at Heythrop College and had also been an Instructor of Tertians at St Beuno's in North Wales.

Pope Pius XI died on 10 February 1939, and Pope Pius XII was elected on 2 March. Fr Geddes always maintained dignified links with Rome and on the Feast of St Ignatius that year Pontifical High Mass was celebrated in great splendour at Farm Street by Archbishop William Godfrey, the first Apostolic Delegate to Great Britain. The following year the Archbishop was again at Farm Street, when he preached on 'The Enthronement of the Sacred Heart in the Home'. This was a very different occasion from his first visit, for Britain was now at war with Germany. In anticipation of air raids the Writers' Library was moved to Roehampton and the church's beautiful north chancel window was carefully dismantled and packed in a cellar.

In June 1940 the air raids began in earnest. Buckingham Palace was hit in September, and pictures of the King and Queen standing before their damaged home occasioned Queen Elizabeth's famous remark, 'Now I can look the East End in the face' (fig. 81). Farm Street was bombed fifty-seven days in succession. The cellars of 114 Mount Street were used as night shelters and the people of Mayfair huddled together in them. The area around Curzon Street and Berkeley Square was particularly vulnerable, as from 1939 Leconfield House had been under construction there. *The Times* had nonchalantly described it as an office block, which was to include air-raid shelters, but it was in fact the new purpose-built headquarters of MI5, the defensive arm of the British Intelligence Service. There were no windows on the ground floor and it was rumoured that underground passages led from the basement to Buckingham Palace.

On 16 September 1940 a bomb fell in Mount Street, but did not explode. On 18 September the church roof was hit (fig. 82), and a chain of water buckets was organised to stop the fire from spreading. Chalices and vestments were moved to safety at 114 Mount Street. From the following day all Masses were celebrated in the Sodality Hall and Chapel. The statues in the west aisle were taken down and stored in the Agony Chapel beside the front entrance. On 21 September a bomb hit the organ loft and on 7 October bombs shattered nearly all

Fig. 83
Private Frank Pakenham (*right*), 1939.
Photographer unknown

the windows on the garden side of the Community Residence and the confessionals on the Gospel side of the church. These also damaged the window above the high altar. Two days later flying debris from a house in Farm Street hit the cross and one of the pinnacles over the church's main entrance and the cross over the sanctuary. A bomb that fell on 16 April 1941 shattered all the windows in the Community Residence, while in the church, the rose window, the small windows above the organ loft and the Lourdes window were all blown out. Despite shrapnel damage to the masonry and roof, the Community was still not evacuated, although the Revd P. C. Usher offered the Jesuits the use of the Grosvenor Chapel in South Audley Street.[9] A temporary roof covered with rubber was erected to protect the church, and although it served for the next decade to keep the rain out, it offered little insulation, so that heating became a terrible expense, even after the end of the war, when fuel ceased to be rationed. Masses continued in the Sodality Hall and the Chapel until 1942, by which time the church was in normal use again.

During the war years Farm Street became known as 'the Converts' Church'. Second Lieutenant Frank Pakenham (later Lord Longford; fig. 83) had been taking instruction there from Fr D'Arcy. Evelyn Waugh alleged that he wrote to Pakenham in 1940 that the middle of a war was not the moment to procrastinate: 'This is no time for a soldier to delay.'[10] With his battalion due to be sent overseas and Fr D'Arcy away, Pakenham gained permission to visit the Greyfriars at Iffley and continue his instruction there. In January it transpired that he was to be sent to the Isle of Wight, so he obtained leave to spend a night at the Greyfriars, where he was received into the Catholic Church. He did not mention his conversion to his wife, Elizabeth, who disapproved deeply of Roman Catholicism, having supported the wider use of contraception in a debate at the Oxford Union while an undergraduate. Eventually she forgave him and was herself received into the Catholic Church on Easter Sunday 1946.

During the last stages of the war 'doodlebugs', as the German V1 rockets were known, caused widespread alarm in London, especially after one hit the Guards Chapel in 1944. They were followed by even more terrifying attacks in the last months, when V2s were in use. Although many regular members of the Farm Street congregation were away fighting, the presence of US forces in Grosvenor Square brought American Catholics to Farm Street. General Eisenhower had taken 20 Grosvenor Square as his base, causing the square to be nicknamed 'Eisenhowerplatz', and for many years afterwards the northern side of the square was the US Naval Headquarters, with the huge US Embassy occupying the entire western side. Despite the announcement that the US Embassy is to move to Nine Elms, many American families resident in Mayfair continue nostalgically to regard Farm Street as their parish.

After the war, Fr Geddes was succeeded by Fr Devas (fig. 84), to whom there fell the difficult task of rebuilding. Exceptionally sociable and with a great sense of humour, Fr Devas had

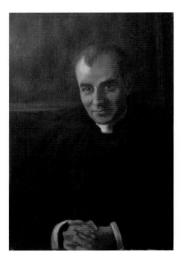

Fig. 84
Fr Francis Devas.
Photographer unknown

Fig. 85
Gavin Maxwell, *Fr Alfred Newman Gilbey*,
1949. Oil on canvas. Fisher House,
Cambridge

Fig. 86
Fr Hubert McEvoy.
Photographer unknown

been a part of the Farm Street team since 1923. He was a popular preacher and a fine spiritual director. In 1946 he replaced the Pulpit Dialogues with Tuesday Talks, aimed particularly at non-Catholics. Fr Thomas Corbishley, Master of Campion Hall, preached on the Feast of the Immaculate Conception to great acclaim. Recruitment of boys for the choir continued to be a problem, as there were still no schools in the area. During the war years the choir had been reduced to a male-voice quintet, but a mixed choir was now formed. In 1947 St Joseph's Library, closed since 1940, was reopened. Fr Devas formally blessed it, and Fr Steuart spoke movingly of its history to a gathering of former subscribers.

The Centenary of Farm Street was celebrated on Sunday 31 July 1949 with great pomp. In an illustrated book by Fr Bernard Basset, Cardinal Bernard Griffin wrote in his foreword: 'To Catholics Farm Street has only one meaning. The Jesuit church enjoys a reputation extending far beyond the confines of the great metropolis in which it plays so important a role.'[11] He presided at the High Mass but on medical advice did not attend the celebratory lunch. In the evening the Bishop of Southwark called to offer his personal congratulations to the Cardinal. In the same year a Sunday Mass for Czech refugees was established in the Sodality Chapel; this continues to the present day. An even greater centenary was celebrated in 1950, which saw the hundredth anniversary of the Restoration of the Catholic Hierarchy in Great Britain. This coincided with a Holy Year of Jubilee. At Farm Street a centenary exhibition was mounted in the Sodality Hall and in July on the Feast of St Ignatius one of the most colourful personalities of twentieth-century Catholicism was invited to give the panegyric. He was not yet known as Monsignor and nor had he reached the zenith of his reputation for amiable eccentricity, but Fr Alfred Gilbey (fig. 85), Roman Catholic Chaplain to the University of Cambridge, undoubtedly spoke wittily and well. By September 1950 Fr Hubert McEvoy (fig. 86) had succeeded Fr Devas as Superior. On 1 November of that year Pope Pius XII defined the Dogma of the Assumption of the Blessed Virgin Mary 'that the Immaculate Mother of God was assumed body and soul into heavenly glory'. This was the first *ex-cathedra* 'infallible' statement issued since the ruling of papal infallibility made by the First Vatican Council in 1869–70. The Pulpit Dialogues were resumed and the church was again filled to capacity. In honour of the new dogma a special luncheon was given by the Sodality of the Immaculate Conception, whose dogma had been defined since 1854. Fr McEvoy wanted to end the year by making the residents of Mayfair more keenly aware of the religious significance of Christmas, and Farm Street became the first London church to put up an outside crib. In 1951, as part of the Festival of Britain, the church organised a Catholic Historical Exhibition, which some 3,000 visitors attended. Reconciled to their mixed status, the choir, directed by Fernand Laloux, sang the choruses at the Scala Theatre in Charlotte Street in performances of Elgar's *The Dream of Gerontius*, while in November American Thanksgiving Day was celebrated at Farm Street for the first time; it has now become an annual event.

During his short period as Superior, Fr McEvoy accomplished the complete renovation of the church and of the two houses attached. The autumn of 1951 saw building licences granted by Westminster Council, which meant that the serious work could begin. The south front was completely redesigned by Adrian Gilbert Scott (see fig. 40). A new roof of handmade tiles replaced the old Welsh slates with their makeshift rubber covering, but during these roof repairs electrical problems arose and new lighting was required. The interior stonework was again cleaned and the roof and sanctuary arch repainted. In due course the high altar was re-gilded and the pews were stripped and revarnished, while the position of the Stations of the Cross was completely changed, so that they no longer obscured the beautiful stonework frieze running along the wall of the Sacred Heart aisle. The church bell was re-cast and the Irish stained-glass artist Evie Hone was commissioned to design a new rose window (fig. 89) as well as the Assumption Window for the Lourdes Chapel (fig. 87). The organ was restored and some new stops were fitted. On 31 August 1952 the bell was solemnly christened by Archbishop Myers, but owing to mechanical complications it could not be rung until November. Luckily it was working by 3 December, the quatercentenary of the death of St Francis Xavier. It also pealed joyously throughout 1953, Coronation Year. Evie Hone's beautiful rose window showing the 41 Instruments of the Passion was completed and unveiled by Archbishop Thomas Roberts in March. Meanwhile, in *Christus Dominus*, Pope Pius XII changed the rule that had hitherto forbidden Mass to be celebrated after 4 pm. The first Evening Mass at Farm Street was celebrated on 1 June, the eve of Queen Elizabeth II's Coronation. Later that year the church was used as the location for a wedding scene in the film *Knave of Hearts*, starring Gérard Philipe, which won an award at the 1954 Cannes Film Festival.

On 29 December 1953 Fr McEvoy was succeeded as Superior by Fr Leo Belton, who had been Rector of Stonyhurst throughout the war. Belton was already well known at Farm Street, and in 1953 Fr Harold Roper and Fr Jan Lang also joined the Community. Known always as Johnnie, Fr Lang had left Czechoslovakia in 1945, having spent part of the war in a concentration camp. He came to England and after 1949 visited Farm Street regularly to say Mass in the Sodality Chapel. He worked tirelessly for the Czech community, broadcasting regularly to Czechoslovakia in 'London Calling Europe', a series of programmes run by the BBC's Overseas Service. A jovial, bustling figure, he knew the names of all his flock and was forever organising dances and encouraging young people to be sweethearts. In the late 1950s he was officially put in charge of all Czech refugees in England. Fr Belton continued Fr McEvoy's restoration programme and in 1955 two new windows were erected in St Joseph's Chapel, given by friends of Fr Devas in memory of his thirty years of ministry. A further window had been designed by Evie Hone for the south end of the west aisle to complement her Assumption Window in the Lourdes Chapel. This was to have included scenes from the life of St Ignatius, but she died before she could begin the work. A great deal of ordinary cleaning was also still needed. The painting behind the altar in the

Figs 87, 88
Evie Hone's window of the Assumption
of the Virgin in the Chapel of Our Lady
of Lourdes (*left*). Hone's death in 1955
forestalled plans for further windows
by her, but in 1964 Patrick Pollen, who
inherited her studio, designed a window
(*right*) depicting English martyrs for the
south end of the west aisle.

The south wall of the nave. The
organ, built in 1889, was rebuilt by
Willis in 1926. When it was restored
in 1980 the pipes were decorated
in the style of A. W. N. Pugin. The
statues flanking the door depict St
John Nepomucene (*left and below*),
by Charles Whiffen, and St Anthony
of Padua, by an unknown Italian
sculptor. The stained glass in the rose
window, depicting the Instruments
of the Passion, is by Evie Hone.

Sacred Heart Chapel – the work of the Rhineland painter Peter Molitor – was coated with dirt and grease from candle smoke. It was restored by Maurice Bradell.

The 1950s were a time of constant renewal at Farm Street. On 1 January 1956 new rubrics regulating the order of Masses came into effect. The Maundy Thursday Mass was changed to the evening and the long Good Friday liturgy moved to the afternoon. The Easter Vigil was reformed and moved from the morning to the evening. The year also saw the quatercentenary of the death of St Ignatius. Archbishop Gerald O'Hara, the Apostolic Delegate, celebrated on the saint's feast day and Fr Brodrick gave the panegyric. He had already begun to write his Life of St Ignatius, the first volume of which was published in the centenary year.[12] In August Cardinal Griffin died, and Archbishop William Godfrey was translated from Liverpool to take over at Westminster. The Tuesday Talks for non-Catholics were also given a new lease of life, when Fr Robert Wingfield-Digby streamlined them into 'Tuesday Talks for Enquirers'. The most revolutionary change came in 1957, when the Papal Bull *Sacram Communionem* reduced the long fast from solid food and alcohol to a three-hour abstinence and one hour from water. This came as a relief to many mid-twentieth-century Catholics, whose busy, energetic and frequently urban lives made it difficult to follow practices that had prevailed when the pace of life was slower. Mass times were also changed, leading at Farm Street to the institution of lunch-hour Masses on weekdays and evening Masses on Sundays. The rise in attendance was phenomenal.

Farm Street received great accolades on 2 November 1956, when the *News Chronicle* published a series about 'The Living Church':

It is not a particularly large church and can seat no more than 800 worshippers at any service, yet 78,000 Communions are given there every year. Sunday by Sunday there are seven Masses each morning, beginning at 6.55 and ending at 12 noon – also an afternoon service and an evening Mass. The Roman Catholic clergy recognise it as a great teaching centre for those in spiritual difficulties, or those wishing to be instructed in Roman Catholicism.

The writer went to two Masses. He found them 'thronged and cosmopolitan'. They were attended 'by men and women of every race and class … diplomats and dustmen, socialites and servants'. The choir, he said, was 'memorably magnificent'. He concluded, 'At Farm Street religion is practised on an almost astronomical scale.'[13]

Throughout the 1950s Farm Street's reputation as the Converts' Church continued. On 4 August 1955 it was dramatically enhanced by the 'defection to Rome' of the poet Edith Sitwell (fig. 91). Evelyn Waugh recorded in his diary: '11.45 to Farm Street where I met Fr Darcy [*sic*] and went with him to the church to the Ignatius chapel to await Edith … A bald, shy man introduced himself as the actor Alec Guinness. Presently Edith appeared swathed in black like a sixteenth-century infanta ... Edith recanted her errors in fine ringing tones and received conditional baptism, then was led into the confessional while six of us collected in the sacristy ... We drove two streets in a large hired limousine to Edith's club, the Sesame ... Edith had ordered a banquet – cold consommé, Lobster Newburg, steak, strawberry flan and great quantities of wine.'[14] In October she was confirmed at Farm Street. Waugh's diary records Elizabeth Pakenham's complaint that Archbishop Roberts treated the congregation like schoolchildren: 'Now I want you all to learn a very useful prayer ... Repeat after me,' he had said condescendingly.[15]

Fr Thomas Corbishley of Campion Hall succeeded Fr Belton as Superior in 1958, when many repairs were still needed. During 1959 the church lighting was again renewed, and at 114 Mount Street and 31 Farm Street hot and cold water was installed in all the bedrooms. The Writers' Library was reorganised for the first time since the war, while in November St Joseph's Library was closed and its books were taken to the Central Catholic Library in Wilfred Street.[16] By 1960 the exterior stonework of the church had to be refaced. In 1965 the floor of the Sanctuary was repaved in marble and a unique innovation was introduced: sound-proof glass walls were erected around the Chapel of St Ignatius to prevent wailing babies from disturbing the congregation during Mass (wits among the resident clergy occasionally refer to the chapel as 'Screamers' Corner').

There remained one significant omission. The Church of the Immaculate Conception had never formally been made a parish church. On 1 January 1966 it at last became one. On 28 January there was a concelebrated Low Mass for the induction of its Parish Priest, Fr Robert Brooks. Cardinal John Heenan was the principal celebrant and the twelve concelebrants were five Jesuit fathers and seven priests from the cathedral and adjacent parishes. Monsignor Gilbey was present and four Anglican priests also attended. The Cardinal's homily emphasised that this new development for Farm Street was in the spirit of Vatican II. Afterwards there was a reception at the Washington Hotel. The church was now a place in which weddings and baptisms could be held. A font was placed in the Calvary Chapel, although nowadays a moveable font is used so that baptisms can take place nearer the Sanctuary. M. Laloux had retired as Choirmaster in 1964, and three years later Guy Weitz retired after fifty years as Organist. Nicholas Danby, his most famous student, replaced him and there were new musical opportunities as weddings now abounded. Farm Street's reputation as a fashionable church was enhanced by its proximity to excellent hotels in which receptions could be held. The wedding that attracted most media attention took place in December 1967, when Lady Rachel Pakenham married Kevin Billington, who had made a film about Cardinal Heenan entitled *The English Cardinal*. Fr Agnellus Andrew, who ran the Catholic Centre for

Fig. 91
Dame Edith Sitwell, November 1952. Photograph Terry Fincher, Keystone Press Agency. Hulton Archive Collection

Fig. 92
Lady Antonia Fraser and
Harold Pinter, 19 November
1976 (detail). Photograph Ron
Frehm. Press Association

Broadcasting, officiated. Present were the Cardinal, Fr D'Arcy (who had instructed the bride's father, Lord Longford, who was by that time Leader of the House of Lords) and a full complement of grandchildren. His eldest daughter, Lady Antonia Fraser (fig. 92), was later to convalidate her marriage to Harold Pinter at Farm Street. They had lived together since 1975, and on 27 November 1980 were married in the Kensington Registry Office. Their union was to last thirty-three years until Pinter's death in 2008. Catholic marriage was made possible by the death of Antonia's first husband, Sir Hugh Fraser, in 1984; Pinter's wife, the actress Vivien Merchant, had died in 1972. The couple hesitated from respect for Harold's parents, who had been upset by the timing of his first wedding, which he had absent-mindedly arranged on Yom Kippur, the Jewish Day of Atonement. The Pinters' wedding, described by Antonia as 'the happiest day of my life' and by Harold as a ceremony of 'grave simplicity', was celebrated on the bride's 58th birthday in the Sodality Chapel, which the couple were delighted to find had been used during the war for the Czech refugees' Masses.[17] She carried a bouquet of white roses, freesias and myrtle, grown from a sprig in her mother's wedding bouquet.

In 1973 Fr Kevin O'Callaghan followed Fr Brooks as Parish Priest. The Agony Chapel was made into a bookshop and repository at this time. Then Fr Peter Knott arrived, combining for the first time the offices of Superior of the Community and Parish Priest. He remained until 1984 and was affectionately known as the 'Painter-Priest'. A talented artist and a notable fundraiser, he gave four exhibitions during his time at Farm Street. His pen-and-ink sketch of the church entrance in Mount Street Gardens (fig. 93) still captures perfectly the *rus in urbe* situation of our beautiful church, and is frequently used as a postcard, or a logo. His responsibilities at Farm Street would have daunted a lesser spirit, for as well as his pastoral work, he inherited the ongoing burden of repairs and running costs. 'In 1977', he remembers, 'the roof was falling in and we had a plywood altar. It was not even covered by a frontal. Since Vatican II, which brought in the idea of standing to receive Communion, no one was very sure where altars were meant to be. The roof repairs were estimated at £1,000,000. We had about £5,000 in the kitty! The organ had to be rebuilt, manual work of great complexity. I got a Jesuit brother from Malta to come over, an expert in such matters.'

The money flowed in miraculously. 'I was greatly encouraged when someone sent in £1,000. Then the Editor of *Das Spiegel*, who used to come in and light a candle from time to time, sent a cheque for £10,000. It became quite the thing to "give to Farm Street". The great and famous joined in. It helped that we were near the Connaught, where David Niven and other celebrities stayed. Alec Guinness gave money. Rees-Mogg contributed as did Princess Grace of Monaco. The greatest coup was when an American banker was planning a major operation in North Sea oil. Three partners had to be set up. It was stipulated that one should be a charity. We were to receive 1% of an oil company's profit. I had quite a tussle with our Finance Direc-

Farm Street Church, London

tor about the ethics of accepting. To accord with Vatican II, the trench and gates were moved in the Sanctuary. The lectern was moved and the paintings restored.'[18] Fr Knott always felt he had 'a fine team'. Nicholas Danby was his Organist; sung Latin Mass was instituted as soon as it was reintroduced and in 1981 David Graham became Assistant Director of Music and Organist. In 1982 it was even possible to clean and restore the paintings in the Sacred Heart Chapel.

When Fr Anthony Nye became Parish Priest and Superior in 1984, he too felt blessed with 'an exceptional team'. After a survey about the problems of homelessness in Central London Fr Vincent Hawe, who arrived in 1987, re-founded the St Vincent de Paul Society. Everyone assumed Fr Hawe was American, but Fr Anthony Meredith remembers that he came from Stoke-on-Trent. His transatlantic accent was due to his having been a businessman in Canada. When war broke out he joined the Canadian Army, and after the war he became a priest. He and Fr Meredith were self-confessed 'sparring partners'. American visitors adored Fr Hawe. Fr Meredith is an Oxford man of great distinction. A meticulous scholar, a witty and outstanding preacher, who counsels with love and jokes, he is also a formidable expert on the Early Church. On the subject of St Gregory of Nyssa, Fr Meredith can even be classed as a world expert. Fr Nye also remembers Mrs Pam Leigh and her assistants, who instituted Coffee after the 11 am Sunday Mass: 'She organised bazaars,' he says, 'and CAMEO (Come and Meet Each Other), a non-denominational club for the elderly. They used to make an annual trip to Eastbourne.'[19] Fr Nye and Brigadier Gordon Viner, Chairman of the Mayfair Residents' Association, often joined their meetings at the Montessori School in Balderton Street; Fr Nye was the bingo caller. His versatility is widely appreciated. He advises the BBC on their television series about Father Brown, G. K. Chesterton's 'detective-priest', and has been known to sing his Bing Crosby impersonation from the pulpit.

His team at Farm Street also included Fr John Tracy, remembered by many as Headmaster of St Aloysius School, Glasgow, although few realise that in his early years as a priest he had been a theatrical chaplain. On 5 September 1987 Fr Tracy was about to celebrate the wedding of Dr John Keet and Maria Jesusa Yujico. As the bride entered the church a mighty thunder-clap sounded. The organist had begun Purcell's *Rondeau from 'Abdelazer'* when a trickle of water ran down the wall. The guests were oblivious to the danger; they had their backs to it. Only the celebrant could see the trickle becoming a rivulet and the rivulet gathering momentum as it approached the main electricity cable. Fr Tracy confessed at the reception at Claridge's that he had 'never prayed so hard in his life'. By the time the congregation embarked upon 'Praise, my soul, the King of Heaven', he was imploring, 'Please Lord, don't let the lights go out.' Another awkward situation occurred in 1988, when so many people wished to attend the Requiem Mass for the famous golfer Sir Henry Cotton that it was decided that tickets should be issued. Wherever he went Sir Henry was accompanied by his faithful dogs Trixie and Dolly. His daughter feared they might not be admitted to the service, so tickets were applied for in the names of 'Lady Patricia

Cotton' and 'Lady Delicia Cotton'; both dogs sat at the back of the church chaperoned by Fiona MacDonald. They wore black bows around their necks and decorously refrained from barking.

In 1991 the London Catalan Society presented to Farm Street a reproduction of the Black Madonna of Montserrat, the statue that had inspired St Ignatius when he was writing his *Spiritual Exercises*. She now stands in the St Ignatius Chapel, with its scenes from the life of the saint. By 1992 Fr Michael Beattie had become Parish Priest and Superior. His first concern was pastoral care. He asked the Bishop's permission to visit all who regularly worshipped at Farm Street and then travelled all over London to meet people in their homes. Shortly after his arrival, he made the startling discovery that because the Church of the Immaculate Conception was not originally a parish church, it had never been consecrated. Cardinal Basil Hume remedied this oversight in 1993. The nave was decorated in 1996 in honour of Our Lady, with elegant mosaics covering the marks where the old gas light-fittings had been. Fr Beattie wanted to extend the theme of the Annunciation shown in the mosaic over the high altar. 'I got an icon painter over from Italy to show us the technique,' he says. 'The words of the Ave Maria were placed inside golden roundels. Tony Berridge created the design and Mrs Filomena Monteiro helped with the mosaics. The pieces were bought from a local art shop. We probably spent less than £100 on the whole lot.'[20] It was Fr Beattie himself, however, who climbed a ladder to do the painting at 6 am every morning, before the church was open.

Pugin's high altar also needed restoration at this time. 'A fibreglass copy was made of the original,' he remembers. 'Dental putty was used for the mould, as it was soft enough not to damage the original carving.' One day Fr Beattie was musing on how he could raise funds to renovate the benches, when an American visitor asked him how much it would cost. 'I told him I had received an estimate for £50,000. Next day a cheque for £52,000 arrived in the post.' Like his predecessors, Fr Beattie felt he was supported by an exceptional team. Nicholas Danby, who had been Organist since 1967, died in 1997, and David Graham, Assistant Director of Music and Organist since 1981, took over, with Martin Parry as Choirmaster. After graduating from the Royal College of Music, David taught there and was later appointed Professor-in-charge-of-the-Organ. The current organ at Farm Street dates from 1914 and includes some stops from the 1880s. It has been cherished by successive generations and was last repaired in 2015.

Fr Michael O'Halloran succeeded Fr Beattie in 1998. He introduced the Family Mass, and, as there were no Catholic schools in the district, arranged immediately for the instruction of children for First Communion. Parents were encouraged to participate. The Parish Council was also revived. Joan Hamnet was a leading personality and became very active in promoting events, including the annual pilgrimage to Walsingham and the Farm Street Picnic. This has escalated from a picnic in Hyde Park, with people sitting on rugs eating sandwiches, to a mighty jamboree in Mount Street Gardens with a brass band, a steel band, a Punch and Judy show,

Fig. 94
The Farm Street Picnic, organised
by the Friends of St George's
with Farm Street Church, 2015.
Photograph Margaret Gold for the
Friends of St George's

Fig. 95
Baroness Stefania von Kories
zu Goetzen. Photograph Bob Safie.
Author's collection

a Pimm's tent and, in recent years, a trampoline of epic proportions (fig. 94). It is a joint affair supported by the Mayfair Library, the Grosvenor Chapel and St George's School.

Fr William Pearsall became Parish Priest and Superior at Farm Street in 2004. He introduced separate music sheets with short biographies of the day's composers. Fr Pearsall studied Greats at Oxford and while training for the priesthood was Organist at Campion Hall. He comes of a musically appreciative family: he is an Esterházy, and in the eighteenth century Haydn was their Kapellmeister. To Professor Malcolm Troup, Director of the Guildhall School of Music and later Head of Music and Senior Lecturer at the City University, Fr Pearsall seemed 'like a rainbow after sunshine'.[21] Professor Troup, knowing of Fr Pearsall's musical abilities, immediately invited him to visit him in Kensington to practise on his Steinway. Fr Pearsall came to Farm Street from Stamford Hill. He is extremely pragmatic, and thinks his best work as Parish Priest was developing the Mount Street Parish Centre, where the Outreach Programme soon included the 'Farm Street Helping Hand'. Churches Together in Westminster also flourished. Fr Pearsall encouraged ecumenical expeditions, including a memorable visit to Westminster Abbey, where the Dean, the Very Revd John Hall, invited Anglicans and Catholics to pray together at the tomb of St Edward the Confessor. Churches Together also received massive publicity when Westminster Council tried to enforce punitive Sunday parking charges. Fr Pearsall promptly enlisted the support of local businessmen, pointing out that shopping would be affected. After a storm in the press, the Council surrendered. When in October 2008 the financial crash came, Farm Street set up 'Mission to Mayfair', an association of bankers and hedge-fund managers who could meet in a Christian environment to help those in financial need. Baroness Stefania von Kories zu Goetzen (fig. 95), a patron of many charities, including the British Red Cross, also brought a new dimension to coffee after Mass at this time. The atmosphere has been likened to 'a champagne party without the need for champagne', and most Sundays a fair number of celebrities foregather. Paul Johnson, former Editor of *The New Statesman*, has been a regular attender at Farm Street since his parents took him there as a schoolboy.

Fr Andrew Cameron-Mowat succeeded Fr Pearsall in 2012. He too is a brilliant musician. On New Year's Day 2015 torrents of beautiful music poured forth from the organ loft. As the Mass ended Fr Nye craved a round of applause 'for our organist'. Most people were astounded to discover he was referring to our exceedingly modest parish priest. Many people regarded Fr Cameron-Mowat's performance that morning as a magnificent exercise in multi-tasking. For

him multi-tasking is almost a way of life. Few of his parishioners were perhaps aware that when he arrived at Farm Street he had not fully retired from his work as Provincial's Assistant for Formation, a role that put him in charge of overseeing the development of all students studying for the priesthood in the British Province. He also taught both liturgical studies and sacramental theology at Heythrop, and in the summer of 2014 he compiled the beautiful liturgy for that college's 400th anniversary, concelebrating with many others at the Carmelite Church in Kensington Church Street on 21 June; Cardinal Vincent Nichols was Principal Celebrant. Three members of the Farm Street team were at that time associated with Heythrop. Fr Christopher Pedley was appointed Librarian there in 2000, but has long since migrated to Farm Street. Fr Dominic Robinson teaches Theology at Heythrop, but the late Fr Joseph Laishley, whose requiem was celebrated at Farm Street on 14 July 2015, was perhaps the most venerable. Ordained in 1966, he took a crash course in Sacramental Theology at Heythrop in 1969. He became pre-eminent in his subject, seeking to rid it of some its dryness and aiming to develop it into three separate branches in which he later instructed many younger priests over several decades.

In addition to teaching and preaching, Fr Dominic has made several fundraising pilgrimages. He keeps fit by playing squash at the Lansdowne Club. In 2014 he responded to the crisis in Syria by leading a group of pilgrims to Monserrat and Monresa, following in the footsteps of St Ignatius to raise money for the Jesuit Refugee Service. He also went to Lebanon to see the refugee camps there. In 2015 Farm Street's efforts were focused on the Bakhita Project, which is named after St Josephine Bakhita, who was sold into slavery as a child and later escaped to Italy to become a nun. She is highly regarded as a patron of victims of human trafficking. At Farm Street money is being collected to build a safe house for such women. Its location is being kept secret to ensure maximum security for those who will eventually live there. The overall target is £360,000, and the project is supported by the Archdiocese of Westminster and the Metropolitan Police. Funds from the Christmas and Easter collections are to go towards Bakhita.

In the run up to the fiftieth anniversary of Farm Street becoming a parish church, new glass doors were fitted inside the building and the front elevation was repaired. Stained glass was cleaned, the organ refurbished and the choir moved temporarily to a side chapel, where a digital organ was briefly installed. The hall was also opened as a night shelter for homeless people referred from the West London Day Centre during the spring and autumn, when other winter shelters were closed. On 8 December, at the Solemnity of the Immaculate Conception, Cardinal Vincent Nichols again celebrated Mass. Afterwards, in true Farm Street tradition, the hall threw open its hospitable doors for a champagne reception. The Farm Street Ball, a glittering occasion at the Lansdowne Club on 30 January 2016, also raised funds for Bakhita. Nearly two hundred tickets were sold, which has ensured that night shelters can be provided for 2016; the remainder of the Ball's proceeds will go towards the safe house.

ENDNOTES

THE HISTORY OF FARM STREET TO 1914
SHERIDAN GILLEY
(Pages 11–29)

The majority of sources concerning the early history of Farm Street are bound into three unnumbered volumes at the Archivum Britannicum Societatis Iesu (ABSI) entitled 'College of St Ignatius: Farm Street Church 1802–1865' (abbreviated in these notes as CSI 1802–65); 'College of St Ignatius: Farm Street and Mount Street 1847–1897' (CSI 1847–97); and 'College of St Ignatius: Farm Street and Mount Street 1849–1914' (CSI 1849–1914).

1   The best short history of the parish is by Fr Harold Roper: *Farm Street Church: Short History and Guide*, London, 1960. I am grateful to Rebecca Somerset of the Jesuit Archives, Farm Street (Archivum Britannicum Societatis Iesu, henceforth ABSI) for her guidance.

2   James William Edmund Doyle (1822–1892). Rosemary Mitchell, *Oxford Dictionary of National Biography* (henceforth *ODNB*).

3   Richard Doyle (1824–1883). Michael Heseltine, *ODNB*.

4   Thomas M. McCoog, '"Est et Non Est": Jesuit Corporate Survival in England after the Suppression,' in Robert A. Maryks and Jonathan Wright (eds), *Jesuit Survival and Restoration: A Global History, 1773–1900*, in *Studies in the History of Christian Traditions*, vol. 178, Leiden, 2015, p. 177.

5   Fr Edward Scott: born 1776, ordained 1816, died 1836. Charles Fitzgerald-Lombard, *English and Welsh Priests, 1801–1914: A Working List*, Downside Abbey, Bath, 1993, p. 221.

6   Fr Randall Lythgoe: born 1793, ordained 1826, died 1855. Fitzgerald-Lombard, 1993, p. 216. Randall was also spelled Randal. Maurice Whitehead, '"Education and Correct Conduct": Randal Lythgoe and the Work of the Society of Jesus in Early Victorian England and Wales', in Sheridan Gilley (ed.), *Victorian Churches and Churchmen: Essays Presented to Vincent Alan McClelland*, Woodbridge, 2005, pp. 75–93.

7   Frederick Lucas (1812–1855). Edward Lucas, *The Life of Frederick Lucas, M.P.*, 2 vols, London, 1887; Sheridan Gilley, 'Frederick Lucas, *The Tablet* and Ireland: A Victorian Forerunner of Liberation Theology', in Stuart Mews (ed.), *Modern Religious Rebels: Presented to John Kent*, London, 1993, pp. 56–87; Patrick Maume, '"Brethren in Christ": Frederick Lucas and Social Catholicism in Ireland', in Oliver P. Rafferty (ed.), *Irish Catholic Identities*, Manchester, 2015, pp. 231–42. See also Thompson Cooper, revised Josef L. Atholz, *ODNB*.

8   Fr John Bird: born 1783, ordained 1808, died 1853. Fitzgerald-Lombard, 1993, p. 205.

9   'Unknown', ABSI, 'College of St Ignatius, Farm Street Church 1802–65' (henceforth CSI 1802–65), folio 9.

10   Fr Thomas Glover: born 1781, ordained 1807, died 1849. Fitzgerald-Lombard, 1993, p. 212.

11   Glover to Lythgoe, 28 December 1839, ABSI, CSI 1802–65, folio 11. Also partly quoted in Fr Francis Edwards, *The Jesuits in England: From 1580 to the Present Day*, London, 1985, p. 178.

12   Fr James Brownbill: born 1798, ordained 1829, died 1880. Fitzgerald-Lombard, 1993, p. 206.

13   Fr Bernard Basset, *The English Jesuits: From Campion to Martindale*, London, 1967, p. 430.

14   Bryan Little, *Catholic Churches since 1823: A Study of Roman Catholic Churches in England and Wales from Penal Times to the Present Decade*, London, 1966, p. 92.

15   Bernard W. Kelly, *Historical Notes on English Catholic Missions*, London, 1907, p. 174.

16   Lythgoe to Thomas Glover, 21 July 1841, ABSI, CSI 1802–65, folio 49.

17   Sir Charles Robert Tempest (1794–1865) of Broughton Hall, Yorkshire, 1st (and last) Baronet. According to a note to Fr Peter Gallwey's tribute to Tempest, he built a chapel and school by his estate at Broughton, school buildings at Skipton and the church and presbytery of the Sacred Heart at Blackpool. Fr [Peter] Gallwey, *Salvage from the Wreck: A Few Memories of Friends Departed, Preserved in Funeral Discourses*, London, 1890, p. 13.

18   Kenelm Henry Digby (1795/96–1880) was a convert and the author of such Catholic Romantic and medievalist works as *The Broadstone of Honour, or, Rules for the Gentlemen of England*, London, 1822, subsequently much enlarged, and *Mores Catholici, or, Ages of Faith*, 11 vols, 1831–42. See Bernard Holland, *Memoir of Kenelm Henry Digby*, London, 1919; Margaret Pawley, *ODNB*.

19   William Henry Francis (Petre), 11th Baron Petre (1793–1850). George Edward Cokayne (ed.), *The Complete Peerage*, vol. X, London, 1945, p. 511.

20   William Joseph (Stourton), 18th Baron Stourton (1776–1846). George Edward Cokayne (ed.), *The Complete Peerage*, vol. XII, London, 1953, pp. 313–14.

21   Possibly the Hon. Henry Constable-Maxwell (1809–1890), who added Stuart to his name on succeeding to the ancient Scottish estate of Traquair on the death of his cousin, the 8th Earl of Traquair.

22   Charles Langdale (1787–1868). Rosemary Mitchell, *ODNB*.

23   Gallwey, 1890, p. 20.

24   'Subscriptions for the Church of the Immac. Conception of the BVM London', ABSI, CSI 1802–65, folios 170–79.

25   Charles Januarius Edward Acton (1803–1847). Dominic Aidan Bellenger and Stella Fletcher, *Princes of the Church: A History of the English Cardinals*, Stroud, 2001, pp. 111–13. See also Thompson Cooper, revised Rosemary Mitchell, *ODNB*.

26   Basset, 1967, p. 428.

27   ABSI, CSI 1847–97, folio 195.

28   'Subscriptions to Church of Imm. Conceptn. in London', ABSI, CSI 1802–65, folio 230, and CSI 1802–65, folio 239.

29   Basset, 1967, p. 428.

30   James Bramston (1763–1836). G. Martin Murphy, *ODNB*.

31   Thomas Griffiths (1791–1847). G. Martin Murphy, *ODNB*.

32   Fr John Bird to Fr Thomas Glover, 3 June 1841, ABSI, CSI 1802–65, folio 38.

33   Griffiths to Lythgoe, 16 June 1841, ABSI, CSI 1802–65, folios 39–41.

34   Lythgoe to Glover, 31 December 1842, ABSI, CSI 1802–65, folio 60.

35   Rescript, 23 April 1843, ABSI, CSI 1802–65, folio 62, with Cardinal Acton's letter dated 25 April 1843, urging Lythgoe to accept it, ABSI, CSI 1802–65, folio 63.

36   Glover to Lythgoe, 30 April 1843, ABSI, CSI 1802–65, folio 66.

37   Lythgoe to Glover, 2 June 1843, ABSI, CSI 1802–65, folio 72.

38   Sir William Lawson (1796–1865), 1st Baronet, of Brough Hall, Yorkshire. Born William Wright, he assumed his mother's maiden name of Lawson.

39   'Petition to his Holiness Pope Gregory XVI from certain lay Catholics of England', 7 May 1844, ABSI, CSI 1802–65, folio 90. Lawson to Lythgoe, 9 May 1844, ABSI, CSI 1802–65, folio 95.

40   Lythgoe to Glover, 2 June 1843, ABSI, CSI 1802–65, folio 72.

41   The Hon. Edward Robert Petre (1794–1853), son of the 9th Lord Petre. Joseph Gillow, *A Literary and Biographical History, or Bibliographical Dictionary, of the English Catholics. From the Breach with Rome, in 1534, to the Present Time*, 5 vols, London, 1885–1902, vol. V, pp. 291–92. Petre's widow became a Sister of Notre-Dame de Namur. See A. M. Clarke, *Life of the Hon. Mrs Edward Petre (Laura Stafford-Jerningham)*, London, 1899, with information on her husband.

42   *The Tablet*, 3 August 1844.

43   William Wareing (1791–1865), Bishop of Northampton from 1840.

44   Thomas Joseph Brown (1798–1880), Bishop of Newport and Menevia from 1850.

45   James Gillis (1802–1864), Vicar Apostolic of the Scottish Eastern District from 1852.

46   Frederick Oakeley (1802–1880). P. J. Galloway, *A Passionate Humility: Frederick Oakeley and the Oxford Movement*, London, 1999. Peter Galloway, *ODNB*.

47   Frederick William Faber (1814–1863). Ronald Chapman, *Father Faber*, London, 1961. Sheridan Gilley, *ODNB*.

48   *The Tablet*, 4 August 1849.

49   Wiseman to Frederick William Faber, 27 October 1852. Wilfrid Ward, *The Life and Times of Cardinal Wiseman*, 2 vols, London, 1897, vol. II, pp. 115–17.

50   'A Return of the Several Particulars to be Enquired into respecting the undermentioned Place of Public Religious Worship', 1 April 1851 (Belgrave District of St George's, Hanover Square), The National Archives, Kew (TNA): HO129/3, folio 86. A surviving book of bench rents at Farm Street for 1849–55 (ABSI, Bench Rents, PC/1/12/5) indicates that between August and December 1849 the income from sittings in the church for Sundays and major feasts totalled £92.16.11, including two small entries for the offertory. The total charges for such sittings (with the occasional special collection) for 1850

were £240.5.4, for 1851 £336.8.2, for 1852 £250.3.11, for 1853 £267.9.3, for 1854 £283.9.11¼ and for 1855 £258.1.10¼, which at least indicate a steady income. I am grateful to Mary Allen for discovering this book. The charges may not include special sittings for those so privileged, and does not indicate that sittings were equally priced, so that it is impossible even for Census Sunday to suggest the individual charge per sitting. It is worth bearing in mind that one could employ a dozen servants for £240 a year in 1850.

51   Richard Mudie-Smith, *The Religious Life of London*, London, 1904, p. 2. The general theme of this volume is the inverse ratio of wealth to church attendance.

52   Mudie-Smith, 1904, p. 108.

53   Charles Booth, *Life and Labour of the People in London*, 17 vols, London, 1902–03.

54   Rosemary O'Day and David Englander, *Mr Charles Booth's Inquiry: Life and Labour of the People in London Reconsidered*, London, 1993, especially 'The "New Booth": The Religious Influences Series', pp. 159–98.

55   Booth, 1902–03, Third Series: *Religious Influences*, vol. 3, *The City of London and the West End*, London, 1902, facing p. 136.

56   Booth, 1902–03, Third Series, vol. 3, p. 100. On the Grosvenor Chapel, see Ann Callender, *Godly Mayfair*, London, 1980.

57   Fr Alexander Charnley: born 1834, ordained 1867, died 1922. Fitzgerald-Lombard, 1993, p. 207.

58   Fr Joseph Bampton: born 1854, ordained 1887, died 1933. Fitzgerald-Lombard, 1993, p. 204.

59   The Charity Organisation Society, which sought to work on a scientific basis to avoid abetting pauperism.

60   'Interview with Reverend Father Charnley of the Chapel of the Jesuits, Church of the Immaculate Conception Farm Street, Roman Catholic Church … 17 February 1899'. LSE Library, BOOTH/B/251, folios 102–07.

61   'Interview with Reverend Father Brenan, Church of Our Lady of the Rosary, Marylebone Road, Roman Catholic Church, 16 February 1899'. LSE Library, BOOTH/B/251, folios 130–39.

62   Fr William Waterworth: born 1811, ordained 1836, died 1882. Fitzgerald-Lombard, 1993, p. 224. Thompson Cooper, revised Leo Gooch, *ODNB*.

63   Fr Henry Mahon: born 1804, ordained 1834, died 1879. Fitzgerald-Lombard, 1993, p. 216.

64   Fr Henry Segrave: born 1806, ordained 1836, died 1869. Fitzgerald-Lombard, 1993, p. 222.

65   Fr Edward Theophilus Hood: born 1808, ordained 1851, died 1886. Fitzgerald-Lombard, 1993, p. 213.

66   *The Catholic Directory* (henceforth *CD*), 1856, pp. 34–35.

67   Fr William Cobb: born 1804, ordained 1837, died 1877. Fitzgerald-Lombard, 1993, p. 208.

68   Fr William Cobb to Wiseman, 14 August 1849, ABSI, CSI 1847–97, folio 20.

69   ABSI, Registers of Confraternity of Bona Mors, 1887–1903, 1903–19.

70 ABSI, Register of Confraternity of Our Lady of Compassion, 1898–1900.

71 *Prayers and Devotional Exercises Used at the Church of the Immaculate Conception, Farm Street, Berkeley Square*, London, 1852: 'Devotion to the Bona Mors', pp. 98–114; 'Confraternity of the Sacred Heart of Jesus', pp. 114–19; 'Confraternity of the Immaculate Heart of Mary for the Conversion of Sinners', pp. 119–23; 'Novena of St Francis Xavier', pp. 124–31.

72 *CD*, 1862, p. 69.

73 *CD*, 1873, pp. 95–96.

74 Fr Robert Whitty: born 1817, ordained 1845, died 1895. Fitzgerald-Lombard, 1993, p. 224.

75 *CD*, 1880, p. 101.

76 *CD*, 1895, p. 106.

77 Fr Peter Gallwey: born 1820, ordained 1852, died 1906. Gallwey was author of *Salvage from the Wreck: A Few Memories of Friends Departed, Preserved in Funeral Discourses*, London, 1890. Fitzgerald-Lombard, 1993, p. 211. See also Geoffrey Holt, *ODNB*.

78 It is not clear which of the successive Lords Arundell this was. It may have been the elderly Henry Benedict (Arundell), 11th Baron Arundel of Wardour (1804–1862), or one of his successors to that title. George Edward Cokayne (ed.), *The Complete Peerage*, vol. I, London, 1945, p. 267.

79 Edward Bellasis (1800–1873). Edward Bellasis, *Memorials of Mr Serjeant Bellasis (1800–1873)*, London, 1893. H. C. G. Matthew, *ODNB*.

80 Lord Walter Talbot Kerr (1839–1927). V. W. Baddeley, revised Paul G. Halpern, *ODNB*.

81 Basset, 1967, p. 430.

82 James Robert Hope-Scott (1812–1873). R. Ormsby (ed.), *Memorials of James Robert Hope-Scott*, 2 vols, London, 1884. G. Martin Murphy, *ODNB*.

83 Leslie continues: 'and returns, never to be heard of again.' Shane Leslie, *Henry Edward Manning: His Life and Labours*, London, 1921, p. 98.

84 Edmund Sheridan Purcell, *Life of Cardinal Manning, Archbishop of Westminster*, 2 vols, London, 1896, vol. II, p. 57.

85 Leslie, 1921, p. 297.

86 Basset, 1967, p. 274.

87 Cecil Chetwynd Kerr (1808–1877), Marchioness of Lothian. Rowan Strong, *ODNB*. See also 'Lady Georgiana Fullerton', in Gallwey, 1890, pp. 233–61. On the influence of the Oxford Movement among female aristocrats, see K. D. Reynolds, *Aristocratic Women and Political Society in Victorian Britain*, Oxford, 1998, pp. 75–78. Some 73 British aristocratic converts to Rome in the nineteenth century are listed in George Edward Cokayne (ed.), *The Complete Peerage*, vol. III, London, 1913, pp. 639–41, although some of these were by intermarriage into Old Catholic families.

88 Charlotte Anne Montagu-Douglas-Scott (1811–1895), Duchess of Buccleuch. Her entry is combined with that of Walter Francis Montagu-Douglas-Scott, her husband, by K. D. Reynolds, *ODNB*.

89 Frances Margaret Taylor (1832–1900). F. C. Devas, *Mother Mary Magdalen (Fanny Margaret Taylor): Foundress of the Poor Servants of the Mother of God*, London, 1927. Sister Mary Campion Troughton SMG, *Life of Mother Foundress*, private. I am grateful to Paul Shaw for this reference. Susan O'Brien, *ODNB*.

90 Fr Joseph Woollett: born 1818, ordained 1852, died 1898. Fitzgerald-Lombard, 1993, p. 225.

91 Fr James Clare: born 1827, ordained 1859, died 1902. Fitzgerald-Lombard, 1993, p. 207.

92 Fr Augustine (or Augustus) Dignam: born 1833, ordained 1867, died 1894. Fitzgerald-Lombard, 1993, p. 209.

93 See Mother Frances Taylor, *Memoir of Father Dignam SJ*, London, 1895.

94 Janet Erskine Stuart (1857–1914). Anselm Nye, *ODNB*.

95 (Mother) Maud Monahan, *Life and Letters of Janet Erskine Stuart, Superior-General of the Society of the Sacred Heart, 1857–1914*, London, 1922, pp. 23–41.

96 Mary Elizabeth Towneley (1846–1922). *Mary Elizabeth Towneley, in Religion Sister Marie des Saints-Anges… A Memoir*, London, 1924.

97 Lady Georgiana Charlotte Fullerton (1812–1885). Kathleen Jaeger, 'A Writer or a Religious? Lady Georgiana Fullerton's Dilemma', in Peter Clarke and Charlotte Methuen (eds), *The Church and Literature: Studies in Church History*, vol. 48, Woodbridge, 2012, pp. 271–82. Solveig C. Robinson, *ODNB*.

98 As we are reminded in Fr Henry James Coleridge, *Life of Lady Georgiana Fullerton, from the French of Mrs Augustus Craven*, 2 vols, London, 1888, p. 1.

99 John Oliver Hobbes was the *nom de plume* of Pearl Craigie (1867–1906). J. M. Richards, *John Oliver Hobbes*, London, 1911. Mildred D. Harding, *Air-Bird in the Water: The Life and Works of Pearl Craigie (John Oliver Hobbes)*, 1996. Mildred D. Harding, *ODNB*.

100 Fr Michael Gavin: born 1843, ordained 1877, died 1919. Fitzgerald-Lombard, 1993, p. 221.

101 Fr M. Gavin, *Memoirs of Father P. Gallwey, with Portrait*, London, 1913, p. 21.

102 Roper, 1960, p. 9.

103 Gavin, 1913, pp. 44–57.

104 Fr Albany Christie: born 1818, ordained 1852, died 1891. Fitzgerald-Lombard, 1993, p. 207.

105 Fr Frederick Hathaway: born 1814, ordained 1857, died 1891. Fitzgerald-Lombard, 1993, p. 212.

106 Fr Henry James Coleridge: born 1822, ordained 1855, died 1893. Geoffrey Holt, *ODNB*.

107 Sir John Taylor Coleridge (1790–1876). David Pugsley, *ODNB*.

108 See footnote 98.

109 Fr John Morris: born 1826, ordained 1849, died 1893. Fitzgerald-Lombard, 1993, p. 218. Fr J. H. Pollen, *The Life and Letters of Father John Morris of the Society of Jesus, 1826–1893*, London, 1896. Rosemary Mitchell, *ODNB*.

110 Fr Joseph Stevenson: born 1806, ordained 1872, died 1895. Fitzgerald-Lombard, 1993, p. 222. Francis Edwards, *ODNB*.

111 David Knowles, 'The Rolls Series', *Great Historical Enterprises and Problems in Monastic History*, London, 1963, pp. 105–06.

112 Fr John Hungerford Pollen: born 1858, ordained 1891, died 1925. Fitzgerald-Lombard, 1993, p. 220.

113 John Hungerford Pollen (1820–1902). Anne Pollen, *John Hungerford Pollen*, 1920. Suzanne Fagence Cooper, *ODNB*.

114 Fr Alfred Weld: born 1823, ordained 1854, died 1890. Fitzgerald-Lombard, 1993, p. 224.

115 Basset, 1967, p. 433.

116 Fr Herbert Henry Charles Thurston: born 1856, ordained 1890, died 1939. Fitzgerald-Lombard, 1993, p. 223. Fr Joseph Crehan, *Father Thurston*, London and New York, 1952. Mary Heimann, *ODNB*.

117 *No Popery: Chapters on Anti-Papal Prejudice*, London, 1930.

118 *The Physical Phenomena of Mysticism*, J. H. Crehan (ed.), London, 1952.

119 *Surprising Mystics*, J. H. Crehan (ed.), London, 1955.

120 George Tyrrell: born 1861, ordained 1891, expelled from the Society in 1906, died 1909. Fitzgerald-Lombard, 1993, p. 223. Nicholas Sagovsky, *ODNB*.

121 Maude Petre, *Autobiography and Life of George Tyrrell*, 2 vols, London, 1912, vol. I, p. 162.

122 Petre, 1912, vol. II, p. 272.

123 Petre, 1912, vol. II, p. 263.

124 Roper, 1960, p. 23, calls him King Carlos, although he ascended the throne only in 1889.

125 Their requiem in London, controversially attended by Edward VII, was not held at Farm Street but at St James's, Spanish Place.

126 Simon Loftus, *The Invention of Memory: An Irish Family Scrapbook, 1560–1934*, London, 2013, p. 355.

127 Christopher J. Wright and Glenda M. Anderson (eds), *The Victoria Cross and the George Cross: The Complete History*, 3 vols, York, 2013, vol. 1, pp. 7–8, 13–14.

128 See, for example, 'Lady Georgiana Fullerton', in Gallwey, 1890, pp. 253–61.

129 Coleridge, 1888, p. 315, mentions in her circle Lady Lothian, Lady Londonderry, the Duchess of Buccleuch, the Duchess of Norfolk, Lady Denbigh, Lady Herbert of Lea, Miss (Emily) Bowles (a close friend of Newman) and the women of various Old Catholic families.

130 Basset, 1967, p. 423.

131 Roper, 1960, p. 13.

132 Fr Charles Dominic Plater: born 1875, ordained 1910, died 1921.

133 C. C. Martindale, *Charles Dominic Plater SJ*, London, 1922.

134 Fr Bernard Vaughan: born 1847, ordained 1880, died 1922. Fitzgerald-Lombard, 1993, p. 223.

135 *The Sins of Society*, London, 1906.

136 C. C. Martindale, *Bernard Vaughan SJ*, London, 1923, p. 82.

137 Vaughan also published *Society, Sin and the Saviour: Addresses on the Passion of Our Lord*, London, 1908.

138 Charles Morley, 'The Man with the Bell and the Cross', in his *London at Prayer*, London, 1909, pp. 17–42.

139 Fr Cyril Martindale: born 1879, ordained 1911, died 1963. Fr Philip Caraman, *C. C. Martindale: A Biography*, London, 1967.

140 'Father John Morris', *The Month*, vol. LXXIX, November 1893, p. 300.

141 Obituary of Father James Clare, *Letters and Notices*, vol. XXVI, July 1902, p. 501.

THE ARCHITECTURE AND FURNISHINGS OF THE CHURCH AND THE ASSOCIATED BUILDINGS IN FARM STREET AND MOUNT STREET
MICHAEL HALL
(Pages 31–91)

My principal debt is to Rebecca Somerset, Archivist of the Jesuits in Britain, who provided a great deal of help and guidance on my visits to the Archivum Britannicum Societatis Iesu (ABSI) at Mount Street. I would also like to thank Fr Anthony Nye and Peter Howell, who both commented in detail on a draft of this chapter; Michael Kerney, who provided information about the church's stained glass; and Alice Worsley, for assistance with research.

Virtually all the rather meagre archival sources for the design and building of the Church of the Immaculate Conception are in the ABSI. The early sources are bound into three unnumbered volumes entitled 'College of St Ignatius: Farm Street Church 1802–1865' (abbreviated in these notes as CSI 1802–65); 'College of St Ignatius: Farm Street and Mount Street 1847–1897' (CSI 1847–97); and 'College of St Ignatius: Farm Street and Mount Street 1849–1914' (CSI 1849–1914). The ABSI also contains drawings relating to the church, but with the exception of those by Romaine-Walker for the west aisle and his proposed rebuilding of the upper parts of the church, these date only from the post-war period.

The church is orientated north–south, with the liturgical east end facing north. Throughout this book the geographical rather than the liturgical points of the compass have been used.

1 *The Tablet*, 12 December 1903.

2 Words written on the paper enclosing the donation: ABSI, CSI 1802–65, folio 9.

3 Thomas Glover to Randall Lythgoe, 28 December 1839. ABSI, CSI 1802–65, folios 11–12. Lythgoe's forename is often spelled Randal in contemporary documents.

4 Randall Lythgoe to Thomas Glover, 29 July 1840. ABSI, CSI 1802–65, folio 34.

5 Randall Lythgoe to Thomas Glover, 17 April 1841. ABSI, CSI 1802–65, folios 36–37. St Mary Moorfields, in Finsbury Circus, was opened in 1820.

6 Details of the agreement are set out in a letter from Randall Lythgoe to Thomas Glover, 14 May 1843, ABSI, CSI 1802–65, folios 67–68.

7 Details of fundraising and expenditure are summarised in ABSI, CSI 1802–65, folios 170–77.

8 Randall Lythgoe to Thomas Glover, 30 May 1840, ABSI, CSI 1802–65, folios 25–26.

9 Randall Lythgoe to the Earl of Shrewsbury, 10 August 1844, ABSI, CSI 1802–65, folios 107–08.

10 The principal modern accounts of Scoles's career are S. J. Nicholl, rev. Peter Howell,

'Joseph John Scoles (1798–1863), Architect', *ODNB*, and the entry in Howard Colvin, *A Biographical Dictionary of British Architects 1600–1840*, 4th edition, London and New Haven, 2008, pp. 908–10.

11 A. W. N. Pugin to E. J. Willson, 1 January 1835, in Margaret Belcher (ed.), *The Collected Letters of A. W. N. Pugin*, vol. 1 (1830–42), Oxford, 2001, p. 46.

12 See the report on the church by Goldie, Child and Goldie, 29 February 1884, ABSI, CSI 1849–1914, folios 51–52.

13 The intention to erect a tower in this position is referred to in a letter from Lythgoe to Thomas Glover, sending tracings of Scoles's drawings (which do not survive), 26 February 1844, ABSI, CSI 1802–65, folio 251.

14 Randall Lythgoe to the Earl of Shrewsbury, 25 April 1844, ABSI, CSI 1802–65, folios 105–06.

15 J. J. Scoles to Randall Lythgoe, 6 September 1844, ABSI, CSI 1802–65, folio 254.

16 The date of 1849 for the print is given in the 1912 *Guide to the Church of the Immaculate Conception...* which also states incorrectly that it was published in *The Builder*. Lythgoe refers to commissioning the print in a letter to the Earl of Shrewsbury, 25 April 1844, ABSI, CSI 1802–65, folios 105–06.

17 *The Morning Post*, 1 August 1849, p. 5. The author of this description attributes the design of the decoration to Pugin, but there is no other evidence for this, and Bulmer was in other instances wrongly associated with Pugin, to Pugin's anger: see Margaret Belcher (ed.), *The Collected Letters of A. W. N. Pugin*, vol. 3 (1846–48), Oxford, 2009, p. 384. Early descriptions of the church do not mention the painting of the Virgin Mary flanked by angels on the chancel arch, suggesting that it was not part of Bulmer's scheme, although it would be surprising to find no decoration there. In its present form, restored after wartime damage, the painting may date from the time of the completion of the west aisle in 1903. Support for this possibility is offered by a trade catalogue of about 1904 published by the ecclesiastical decorators Bell & Beckham, which lists under 'Farm Street Church', 'Decoration of Church Figure and Ornamental Glass'. I am grateful to Michael Kerney for this reference.

18 The description of the clerestory windows is by Francis Bumpus in *The Architect*, 62, 1899, p. 266. I am grateful to Michael Kerney for this reference.

19 *The Illustrated London News*, 4 August 1849, p. 71. Wailes's charge is listed in 'Expenditure to January 1 1851', ABSI, CSI 1802–65, folio 242. Powell's charged £45 and Claudet and Houghton £40 6s 2d. Powell's cashbooks (Victoria and Albert Museum) list two orders for the church, by Scoles for stamped quarries on 18 December 1848, and by the builder, Jackson, for quarries to fill two lights on 6 February 1850 (information from Michael Kerney).

20 A. W. N. Pugin to an unidentified correspondent, probably J. F. Tempest, 23 November 1846, in Margaret Belcher (ed.), *The Collected Letters of A. W. N. Pugin*, vol. 3 (1846–48), Oxford, 2009, p. 170.

21 A. W. N. Pugin to the Earl of Shrewsbury, 13 February 1848, in ibid., p. 440.

22 *The Builder*, 5, 1847, p. 213.

23 *The Ecclesiologist*, 4, 1847, pp. 201–08, at p. 206.

24 *The Builder*, 7, 1849, p. 258.

25 *The Morning Post*, 1 August 1849, p. 5.

26 Note of expenditure on the church to 1 January 1851, ABSI, CSI 1802–65, folio 242.

27 According to Fr Harold Roper, *Farm Street Church: Short History and Guide*, London, 1960, p. 10, the fire occurred at Christmas 1858 and was caused by a candle setting light to the crib. However, in its account of the new chapel, *The Builder* (18, 1860, p. 772) states that the fire occurred at Easter 1859.

28 Molitor's contract, preserved in the archive at Farm Street, ABSI, CSI 1802–65, folio 283, reveals that he was paid £550. This is the only known painting in Britain by this late Nazarene artist; the archive does not explain why he was chosen.

29 Alexander Rottmann, *London Catholic Churches: A Historical and Artistic Record*, London, 1926, pp. 73, 80. In 1861 Phyffers showed Caen stone sculptures of Moses, Elijah and Melchizedek at the Architectural Exhibition in London: they were described by *The Morning Chronicle* (4 April 1861) as being intended for 'the tomb' in the Immaculate Conception. These must be connected with an undated payment listed under expenditure for the Sacred Heart Chapel of £360 for 'Tomb' and 'Sculpture on tomb', ABSI, CSI 1802–65, folio 281. Peter Howell has suggested to me that they may have been figures for a temporary Easter sepulchre.

30 The subject is an interesting iconographical choice for the Sacred Heart: Judah is pleading before Joseph for his brother Benjamin, and offering himself in his place.

31 Drawings by Clutton for both his designs for the east aisle are in the Drawings Collection of the RIBA (PB1478, 1479 and 1480), together with his specification (DB/9/8/1).

32 Invoice from Henry Clutton, 'March 1883', ABSI, CSI 1849–1914, folio 165.

33 The only surviving drawing for this scheme, a plan for a basement under the chapel (RIBA Drawings Collection, PB 1478/5 [14]), may support the idea that the Sodality Chapel is the same as the Chapel of St Ignatius, but its damaged condition makes it difficult to interpret. In his 1960 guidebook (p. 22) Fr Harold Roper states that there was an intention to have a Sodality Chapel on part of what is now No. 31 Farm Street. This may have been an early proposal for what became the Agony Chapel.

34 The indecision about the design of the residence in Farm Street may explain also why Clutton's ambitious proposals for a library and scriptorium in a long range outside the east aisle and running parallel to it were not realised. Drawings relating to this are in the archive of the builders Dove Brothers of London in the Drawings Collection of the RIBA (included in PB 1479), suggesting that Dove had been asked to estimate for them.

35 I can find no reference earlier than Fr Harold Roper's 1960 guidebook to this change, which is not mentioned in Denis Evinson's well-referenced history of the church in his *Catholic Churches of London*, Sheffield, 1998, pp. 41–46.

36 Sheldon Barr, *Venetian Glass Mosaics 1860–1917*, Woodbridge, 2008, p. 125, reproducing a list of Salviati's works published for the World's Columbian Exposition, 1893.

37 ABSI, CSI 1849–1914, folio 5.

38 Payments of £548 to Rattee and Kett for 'Triptych in chapels [sic]' and £1,526 to Samuel Ruddock for unspecified work are listed in a note, 'Expenditure incurred in fitting up the Chapels in the New Aisle', ABSI, CSI 1849–1914, folio 55, but do not record the name of the chapels to which these sums relate.

39 Charles Alphonse Goldie exhibited regularly at the Royal Academy between 1858 and 1879. The side panels of the St Joseph altarpiece (*The Betrothal of the Virgin* and *The Death of St Joseph*) remain in place, but the central painting, *St Joseph*, has been replaced by a sculpture.

40 The builder was Walter Nash and the contract price £9,690, ABSI, CSI 1849–1914, folio 135.

41 George Goldie to Thomas Porter, 21 January 1886, ABSI, CSI 1847–97, folio 269.

42 W. H. Lyall to Thomas Porter, 30 July 1886, ABSI, CSI 1847–97, folio 282.

43 For the history of the site, see 'Mount Street and Carlos Place: Mount Street, South Side', in F. H. W. Sheppard (ed.), *The Survey of London*, vol. 40, *The Grosvenor Estate in Mayfair, Part 2 (The Buildings)*, London, 1980, pp. 326–29. Bentley was also asked to design the new residence in Farm Street, the job later given to Goldie: see Winefride de l'Hôpital, *Westminster Cathedral and Its Architect*, 2 vols, London, 1919, vol. 2, p. 494. I have followed her date of 1872 for the Mount Street design, but in his later correspondence with the church, Clutton states that drawings were submitted in 1876: ABSI, CSI 1849–1914, folio 165. None of Bentley's drawings are known to survive. His only contributions to the church under his own name, relic cupboards made for the sacristy in 1890, have been removed.

44 Purdie lined the chapel with alabaster, to match the chancel and the Sacred Heart Chapel. Either he or the architect of the remodelling of the chancel pierced the chancel's west wall to create a projecting arcade to support part of the organ, matching – but in a different style – what Clutton had done on the east; this feature was left when Romaine-Walker rebuilt this corner of the church, and the arcade now opens into the passage to the north porch.

45 In 1977 the Agony Chapel was converted into a bookshop and repository. Purdie's altar was moved to the Church of the Blessed Sacrament, Copenhagen Street, London, in 2009, as part of a further remodelling of this space to allow a wheelchair ramp to be installed.

46 Copy in ABSI, CSI 1847–97, folio 195.

47 W. H. Romaine-Walker to 'Fr Superior' [Fr John Gerard], 22 October 1898, ABSI, CSI 1849–1914, folios 113–15. In his 1960 guidebook (p. 26), Fr Harold Roper states that the delay was caused also by the lessee of a building on the site refusing on religious grounds to assign her lease to the Jesuits.

48 Ibid.

49 The decision to add the passage and north porch was an afterthought, as these features are not shown in the surviving contract drawings (ABSI) for the church, signed 10 May 1900.

50 The 1912 guidebook (pp. 80–81) illustrates the rails of St Thomas the Apostle's Chapel, and states that they are 'partly old, being a portion of an Italian balustrade'.

51 ABSI, CSI 1849–1914, folio 120, estimate dated 19 August 1904; see also his letter defending the cost, 11 October 1904, ABSI, CSI 1849–1914, folio 122.

52 *The Builder*, 158, 1940, p. 582.

53 'Charles Edward Whiffen', in *Mapping the Practice and Profession of Sculpture in Britain and Ireland 1851–1951*, University of Glasgow History of Art and HATII, online database 2011 (http://sculpture.gla.ac.uk).

54 The statue was paid for by a Mr Eugene Kelly, in memory of his mother; the fact that Mr Kelly's mother's name was Margaret suggests that the subjects of the statues were chosen by the donors. One of the statues, of St Frances of Rome, was carved in Rome in 1906 by the prolific Manx-born sculptor Joseph Swynnerton (1848–1910); the contract (ABSI, CSI 1849–1914, folio 125) states that the architectural elements such as the plinth are to be identical to Whiffen's sculptures, suggesting that Romaine-Walker was still in control. Swynnerton also carved the *Mater Dolorosa* and *Man of Sorrows* in the Calvary Chapel and the statue over the Altar of the Seven Dolours.

55 W. H. Romaine-Walker to 'Fr Superior' (Fr John Gerard), 19 October 1904, ABSI, CSI 1849–1914, folio 123. Julia Gambardella was a daughter of the Italian portrait painter Spiridone Gambardella (c. 1815–1886), who spent most of his career in England. Tayler's cycle of seven paintings for the Chapel of St Ignatius at the Church of the Sacred Heart were paid for with a bequest in 1902. He is otherwise remembered for being an associate of the Newlyn School of painters. I am grateful to Peter Howell for help concerning Tayler's association with the Jesuits.

56 The lost perspective of the design is illustrated in Bernard Basset, *Farm Street*, London, 1948, p. 11.

57 The altar rail survives *in situ*, but its gates were moved to the Calvary Chapel as part

of the reordering of the chancel in the 1980s.
58 Wailes's glass was given to a church in Canada that I have been unable to identify: ASBI contains photographs of it being installed in its new home, inscribed 'St Agnes, Lake Majestic?'. In 1884 Hardman had supplied a window ordered by Purdie for the Lourdes Chapel, which is illustrated in the 1912 guidebook (pp. 52–53).
59 For a detailed account of the 1987 work, see Tim Gough, 'Farm Street Church, London', *Church Building*, Autumn 1990, pp. 35–37, which includes an interesting analysis of the structure of Scoles's roof. The painted decoration is described in *Church Building*, Summer 1987, pp. 86–87. Advice on the decoration was provided by a member of the church's clergy, Fr Anthony Nye.
60 *The Tablet*, 4 January 1997, p. 12.

FARM STREET BETWEEN THE WARS AND BEYOND
MARIA PERRY
(Pages 93–113)

1 Cardinal Newman, as quoted in Maria Perry, *Knightsbridge Woman*, London, 1995, p. 8.
2 'News from the Dioceses. Westminster: The Cardinal's Engagements. Farm Street: The Crib', *The Tablet*, 25 December 1920, p. 26.
3 Quoted in Fr Harold Roper, *Farm Street Church: Short History and Guide*, London, 1960, pp. 45–46.
4 Fr James Brodrick: *The Origin of the Jesuits*, London, 1940, and *St Francis Xavier*, London, 1956.
5 Ernest Newman, quoted in Fr Harold Roper, *Farm Street Church: Short History and Guide*, London, 1960, p. 49.

6 Evelyn Waugh, Entry for Monday 7 July 1930, in Michael Davie (ed.), *The Diaries of Evelyn Waugh*, London, 1979, p. 320.
7 Evelyn Waugh, Entry for Tuesday 8 July 1930, in ibid., p. 320.
8 Fr Harold Roper, *Farm Street Church: Short History and Guide*, London, 1960, p. 51.
9 Ibid., p. 53.
10 Peter Stanford, *The Outcast's Outcast: Lord Longford*, London, 2003, p. 113. The Pakenham family feel that this was an exaggeration on Waugh's part.
11 Fr Bernard Basset, *Farm Street*, London, 1948, p. 1, foreword by Cardinal Bernard Griffin.
12 See note 4.
13 'The Living Church', *News Chronicle*, 2 November 1956.
14 Evelyn Waugh, Entry for Thursday 4 August 1955, in Michael Davie (ed.),

The Diaries of Evelyn Waugh, London, 1979, p. 735.
15 Evelyn Waugh, Entry for Sunday 9 October 1955, in Michael Davie (ed.), *The Diaries of Evelyn Waugh*, London, 1979, p. 745.
16 The Central Catholic Library is currently moving to the University of Durham.
17 Lady Antonia Fraser, *Must You Go? My Life with Harold Pinter*, London, 2010, p. 194.
18 Fr Peter Knott in conversation with the author, 21 February 2015.
19 Fr Anthony Nye in conversation with the author, 2015.
20 Fr Michael Beattie in conversation with the author, 21 February 2015.
21 Professor Malcolm Troup in conversation with the author, March 2015.

FURTHER READING

Simon Bradley and Nikolaus Pevsner, *The Buildings of England: London 6. Westminster*, New Haven and London, 2003

Denis Evinson, 'The Church of the Immaculate Conception, Farm Street', in his *Catholic Churches of London*, Sheffield, 1998, pp. 41–46

Fr Francis Edwards, *The Jesuits in England: From 1580 to the Present Day*, London, 1985

F. H. W. Shepherd (ed.), *The Survey of London*, vol. 40, *The Grosvenor Estate in Mayfair (Part 2): The Buildings*, London, 1980

Fr Bernard Basset, *The English Jesuits: From Campion to Martindale*, London, 1967

Fr Harold Roper, *Farm Street Church: Short History and Guide*, London, 1960

Fr Bernard Basset, *Farm Street, London*, London, 1948

Guide to the Church of the Immaculate Conception…, London, 1912

PHOTOGRAPHIC ACKNOWLEDGEMENTS

All works of art reproduced appear by kind permission of the owners. Every attempt has been made to trace the photographers of works reproduced.

Archivum Britannicum Societatis Iesu: figs 27, 77, 82, 84 and 86.

Fisher House, University of Cambridge © Estate of Gavin Maxwell: fig. 85.

Courtesy of the Friends of St George's, photo Margaret Gold: fig. 94.

Getty Images, London: figs 16, 78 (Hulton Archive), 81 (Universal History Archive) and 91 (Keystone Agency Ltd).

Peter Knott SJ, by kind permission: fig. 93.

Photo after Elizabeth Longford, *The Pebbled Shore*, London (Weidenfeld & Nicolson), 1986: fig. 83.

Mary Evans Picture Library, London: figs 28, 29 (both *Illustrated London News*), 34 ; 76 (*Süddeutsche Zeitung*).

The National Archives, Kew, HO129/3, folio 86: fig. 7.

National Portrait Gallery, London: figs 17 and 19.

National Trust Photo Library: fig. 5.

© Press Association Images: fig. 92.

Royal Welch Fusiliers Regimental Museum, Caernarfon: fig. 31.

Courtesy Bob Safie: fig. 95.

The Sisters of Notre-Dame de Namur: fig. 21.

SMG Congregational Archive, St Mary's Convent, Brentford, reproduced courtesy of the Generalate of the Poor Servants of the Mother of God: fig. 20.

Stonyhurst Archives, by kind permission of the Governors: fig. 14.

The Board of Trinity College Dublin: fig. 55.

Photographs by Andrew Twort: with kind permission of the Church of the Immaculate Conception, Farm Street, and documents and photographs additionally with kind permission of the Archivum Britannicum Societatis Iesu: dust jacket, pages 2, 4–5, 6–7, and figs 1–4, 6, 8–13, 15, 18, 22–26, 32–33, 35–37, 38 (by permission of Williams and Winkley), 39–54, 56–75, 79–80, 87–90.

INDEX

Page numbers in *italics* refer to illustrations and their captions

Achilli, Fr Giacinto 23
Acton, Cardinal Charles 13, *14*, 15
Actors' Interval Club 97
Andrew, Fr Agnellus 108
Anstey, Frederick 66, *68*
Anthony of Padua, St *107*
Archconfraternity of Our Lady of
　　Compassion 19
Arcos, Mme d' *26*, 27, 93

Bakhita, St Josephine 113
Bakhita Project 113
Bampton, Fr Joseph 18, *18*
Barry, Charles 51
Basset, Fr Bernard 24, 102
Bavarian Embassy Chapel, Warwick
　　Street, London 14
BBC 103, 110
Beattie, Fr Michael 87, 111
Beauvais Cathedral 37, 39
Becket, St Thomas 23
Bellasis, Serjeant 20
Belloc, Hilaire 95
Belton, Fr Leo 103, 108
Benedict XV, Pope 94
Bentley, John Francis 51, 68
Berkeley, William, Lord Segrave 33
Berkeley Estate 14, 33, 68
Bernadette Soubirous, St 13
Berridge, Tony 111
Bethnal Green, London 31–3
Billington, Kevin 108
Bird, Fr John 11, *12*, 31, 33
Bissing, Baroness von *74*
Black Madonna of Montserrat 111
Blackburn 11–13
Bona Mors Confraternity 19
Booth, Charles 18–19
Bourne, Cardinal Francis 96, 97
Bradell, Maurice 107
Bramston, Bishop James 14
British Weekly 17
Britten, James 24
Broadbent, Hastings, Reid & New 87
Brodrick, Fr James 95, 107
Brompton Oratory, London 17, 19, 93
Brooks, Fr Robert 108, 109
Brown, Joseph, Bishop of Wales 17
Brownbill, Fr James 13, *13*, 17, 20, 21
Buccleuch, Charlotte, Duchess of 21
Buckfast, Abbot of 97
Buckingham Palace 100
Buckler, John *20*
The Builder *36*, 39, 48, 65, *65*, 75
Bulmer, Henry Taylor 43
Burges, William 51
Burgos Cathedral 72, *76*

CAMEO (Come and Meet Each Other) 110
Cameron-Mowat, Fr Andrew 112–13
Campion, Edmund 96
Canisius, St Peter 95
Carlisle Cathedral 39, *91*

Carlos, Prince of Portugal 27
Carpenter, R. C. 37
Cathedral of the Immaculate Conception,
　　Guyana 66
'The Catholic Church and Social Reform'
　　conferences (1936) 97
Catholic Encyclopaedia 24
Catholic Guild of Israel 94
Catholic Historical Exhibition (1951) 102
Catholic Relief Act (1829) 11
Catholic Social Guild 29
Catholic Students' Society 95
Catholic Truth Society 24
Central Catholic Library, Wilfred Street
　　108
Chambiges, Martin 37
Charnley, Fr Alexander 18, *18*
Chertier, Alexandre 66
Chesterton, G. K. 95, 110
Christie, Fr Albany 23, 24
Christus Dominus 103
Church of England 23
Church of the Immaculate Conception,
　　Farm Street, London
　　Agony Chapel 58, 60, 68, 100
　　anonymous donation to 11–13, 31
　　architects 31, 33–4
　　Blessed Sacrament Chapel 43, 51
　　Calvary Chapel 72, 75, *78–80*, *88–9*,
　　　97, 108
　　Centenary 102
　　chancel *46–7*, 58–60, *59*, 87
　　Chapel of the English Martyrs *92*, 98–9
　　Chapel of Our Lady and St Stanislaus
　　　76–7, *84–5*
　　Chapel of Our Lady of Lourdes 58,
　　　60–5, *62*, 66, *68–9*, 87, 103–7, *104*
　　Chapel of St Aloysius 60, *63*
　　Chapel of St Francis Xavier 60, *64*, 65
　　Chapel of St Ignatius 43, 58, 68, 72,
　　　73–5, *84*, 108, 111
　　Chapel of St Joseph 60, *61*, 65, 103
　　Chapel of Seven Dolours 72–5, *81*
　　choir 96, 97, 100, 102–3, 108, 111, 113
　　church festivals 60
　　clerestory windows 37, 41, 43
　　clergy 19, 20, 29, 102–3, 109, 110–13
　　concern for the poor 27–9
　　confessionals 72–5, 101
　　congregations 17–18
　　consecration 111
　　construction 17, 31
　　converts 20, 21–4, 96–7, 101, 107–8
　　design 34–41, *35*, *42*
　　east aisle 39, 58
　　establishment of 11–15
　　finances 13–14, 15, 19, 33–4, 48, 68–71,
　　　72–5, 96, 109–10, 111
　　furnishings and decoration 41–9, 60
　　high altar 13, 43–8, *46–7*, 87, 101, 103,
　　　111
　　Masses 17, 19, 107
　　military connections 27

mosaics *43*, *49*, 60, 87, 111
nave 41–3, *106*
north front 39, *40–1*
opening of 17, 48
organ 41, 48, 96, 103, *106*, 109, 111, 112,
　　113
Outreach Programme 95
parochial status 33, 108, 111
Pulpit Dialogues 94–5, 102
renovation 103, 108, 113
Rescript of 23 April 1843 15, *16*
residence 13, 65–6, *65*, *67*, 101
roof 41, 87, 103, 109
royal connections 27
Sacred Heart Chapel *50*, *52–7*, *51–8*, 103,
　　107, 110
Sanctuary 108, 110
site 31–3, *32*
Sodality Chapel 100, 101, 102, 103, 109
south front *36*, 37–9, *38*
stained glass 43, 48, *49*, *62*, 87, *90–1*,
　　103–7, *104*, 113
Stations of the Cross 103
subscribers 13–14, 33
Tuesday Talks 102, 107
weddings 108–9
west aisle 31, 39, 41, 58, 68–75, 100,
　　76–7
Churches Together in Westminster 112
Clare, Fr James 21, *21*, 29
Claudet and Houghton 43
Clutton, Henry *50*, 51–8, *58*, 60, 60, 65,
　　65, 72
Cobb, Fr William 19, *19*
Coleridge, Fr Henry James 23, 24
Coleridge, Sir John Taylor 23
Columbia (recording company) 97
Confraternity of the Sacred Heart 21
Congregation of Propaganda Fide 15
Connaught Hotel, London 109
Corbishley, Fr Thomas 102, 108
Cotton, Sir Henry 110–11
Counter-Reformation 17, 34, 39–41
Coward, Noël 96
Crace, J. G. & Son 60
Crosby, Bing 110
Czechoslovakia 103, 109

Daily News 17
Danby, Nicholas 108, 110, 111
D'Arcy, Fr Martin 96, *96*, 97, 101,
　　108, 109
Daughters of the Heart of Mary 93–4
Day, Fr Arthur 94
Della Robbia workshop
　　Madonna and Child *10*, *92*
Derby, 17th Earl of 72
Desanges, Louis William
　　*Sergeant Luke O'Connor Winning His
　　　VC at the Battle of the Alma* *28*
Devas, Fr Francis 97, 101–2, *102*, 103
Devonshire, 9th Duke of 72
Digby, K. H. 13

Dignam, Fr Augustus 21
Donnelly, Fr Terence 93, 94
Doyle, Sir Arthur Conan 11
Doyle, James 11
Doyle, Richard ('Dick Kitcat') 11, 20
Driscoll, Fr John 96
Dublin Eucharistic Congress 97
Dublin Review 41
Duchêne, Achille 72
Dürer, Albrecht *76*

Earp, Thomas 51, *51*, 66
Ecclesiological Society 48
The Ecclesiologist 48
Edward, Prince of Wales 27
Edward the Confessor, St 112
Eisenhower, General Dwight D. 101
Elgar, Edward
　　The Dream of Gerontius 102
Elizabeth, Queen 100, *100*
Elizabeth II, Queen 103
Ely Cathedral 23
English Decorated style 41, 58
English Martyrs, Streatham 68
Eugénie, Empress *26*, 27, 93

Faber, Fr Frederick William 17
Farm Street Ball 113
'Farm Street Helping Hand' 112
Farm Street Picnic 111–12, *112*
Farmer and Brindley 63, 66
Festival of Britain (1951) 102
First Vatican Council (1869–70) 102
First World War 93–4
Fisher, St John 97
Flanders 14
Florence 75
Franchi of Clerkenwell 51, *51*
Francis Xavier, St 23, 75, 95, 103
Fransoni, Cardinal James 13
Franz Ferdinand, Archduke 27, 93
Fraser, Lady Antonia 109, *109*
Fraser, Sir Hugh 109
French Flamboyant style 72
French Gothic architecture 51
Fullerton, Lady Georgiana 21–3, *22*, 27

Gainsborough, 2nd Earl of 21
Gallagher, Fr George 97, 100
Gallini sisters 14
Gallwey, Fr Peter 20, *20*, 21–3, 25, 27, 60
Galton, Fr Charles 94, 95
Gambardella, Julia 75, *76*, *80*
Gandhi, Mahatma 96
Gavin, Fr Michael 21
Geddes, Fr Leonard 100–1
George VI, King 100, *100*
Gerard, John 23
Gérôme, Jean-Léon 75
Gesù, Rome 39
Gigli, Beniamino 97
Gilbey, Monsignor Alfred 102, *102*, 108
Gill, Eric *92*

Gillis, James 17
Gladstone, William Ewart 20
Glover, Fr Thomas 13, 31–3
Godfrey, Archbishop William 100, 107
Goldie, Charles 60, 65, *65*
Goldie, Child and Goldie 65
Goldie, Edward 60, 65
Goldie, George 39, 60–6, 65, 67, 68
Gothic architecture 34, 37, 51
Grace, Princess of Monaco 109
Graham, David 110, 111
Gregory XVI, Pope 15
Gregory of Nyssa, St 110
Griffin, Cardinal Bernard 102, 107
Griffiths, Bishop Thomas 14, 17, 31–3
Grosvenor Chapel, London 18, 112
Grosvenor Estate 18, 68
Grosvenor Square, London 101
Guinness, Alec 107, 109

Hall, Very Revd John, Dean of
    Westminster 112
Hamnet, Joan 111
Hardman of Birmingham 48, *49*, 87, *91*
Harker, Phil 95
Harnack, Adolf von 25
Hathaway, Fr Frederick 23, 24, 27, *29*
Hawe, Fr Vincent 110
Hayes, Fr James 68
Heenan, Cardinal John 108
Heythrop College, London 113
Hicks, Fr Leo 95
Hill, William (organ builder) 48
Hobbes, John Oliver (Mrs Craigie) 21
Hohenburg, Sophie, Duchess of 93
Hone, Evie *62*, 87, 103–7, *104*, *106–7*
Hood, Fr Edward T. 19
Hope-Scott, James 20, 21
House of Writers 24
Hudson, R. W. 72
Hume, Cardinal Basil 111

Ignatius Loyola, St 37, *82*, 95, 107, 113
    Spiritual Exercises 97, 111
The Illustrated London News 43
Immaculate Conception, dogma of 13
Immaculate Conception Charity 21–3
Inge, William 95
Ireland 14, 27, 39
Ireland, Joseph 34

Jackson, William 48
Jarrett, Fr Bede 94, 95
Jesuit Refugee Service 113
Jesuits see Society of Jesus
John Nepomucene, St *107*
Johnson, Paul 112

Keet, Dr John 110
Kerr, Lord Walter 20
Klinger, Max 75
Knave of Hearts (film) 103
Knott, Fr Peter 109–10, *110*

Knox, Fr Ronald 94
Kories zu Goetzen, Baroness Stefania
    von 112, *112*
Kostka, St Stanislaus *84*

Laishley, Fr Joseph 113
Laloux, Fernand 96, 102, 108
Lang, Fr Jan (Johnnie) 103
Langdale, Hon. Charles 13, 15, 20
Lawson, Sir William, Bt 15
Legros, Pierre *84*
Leigh, Pam 110
Leslie, Shane 20
Lille Cathedral 51
London Catalan Society 111
Longford, 7th Earl of (Frank Pakenham)
    101, *101*, 109
Lothian, Cecil Chetwynd Kerr, Dowager
    Marchioness of 20, 21, *21*
Louis Napoléon, Prince Imperial 25, *25*
Lourdes 13
Lucas, Frederick 11
Lyall, William 65, 66, *68*
Lyons 14
Lythgoe, Fr Randall 11, *11*, 13, 15, 21, 31–4,
    37, 39, 41, 48, 51

MacDonald, Fiona 111
McEvoy, Fr Hubert 102–3, *102*, 103
McQuoid, Percy 95
Madame Tussaud's, London 94
Mahon, Fr Henry 19, *19*
Maidstone 39
Manning, Cardinal Henry Edward 20–1,
    20, 23, 24, 29
Mantegna, Andrea *80*
Margaret of Scotland, St 75, *82*
Marianism 13
Marlborough, 9th Duke of 72
Martindale, Fr Cyril 29, *29*, 95
Martyrs of Paraguay 97
Martyrs of South America 97
Maxwell, Gavin *102*
Maxwell, Henry 13
Mayer & Co. *30*
Mayfair Library 112
Mayfair Residents' Association 110
Merchant, Vivien 109
Meredith, Fr Anthony 110
The Messenger of the Sacred Heart 23
MI5 100
Millais, Sir John Everett
    Cardinal Newman 21
'Mission to Mayfair' 112
Molitor, Peter 51, *51*, 107
Monteiro, Filomena *43*, 87, 111
The Month 21, 23, 24
Morani, Vincenzo
    Cardinal Charles Acton 14
More, St Thomas 97, *97*
The Morning Post 43, 48
Morris, Fr John 23, *23*, 24, 29
Mount Street Parish Centre 112

Mount Street presbytery, London 66, 68,
    70–1
Murphy, Belinda 27
Myers, Archbishop 103
Myers, George 34, 48

Newman, Ernest 96
Newman, Cardinal John Henry 17, 20, 21,
    23, 24, 34, 93
News Chronicle 107
Nichols, Cardinal Vincent 113
Nicholson, Fr Charles 93
Niven, David 109
Nye, Fr Anthony 110, 112

Oakeley, Frederick 17
O'Callaghan, Fr Kevin 109
O'Connor, Sir Luke 27, *28*
O'Halloran, Fr Michael 111
O'Hara, Archbishop Gerald 107
Oratorians 34
Order of Christ 15
Our Lady, St John's Wood, London 37
Our Lady of Farm Street *30*, *49*
Our Lady Help of Christians, Blackheath,
    London 68
Our Lady of the Rosary, London 19
Oxford Group 97
Oxford Movement 23, 24
Oxford Union 101

Pakenham, Elizabeth, Countess of
    Longford 101
Pakenham, Frank, 7th Earl of
    Longford 101, *101*
Pakenham, Lady Rachel 108–9
Paraguay 97
Parry, Martin 111
Pate, Thomas 66
Pearsall, Fr William 112
Pedley, Fr Christopher 113
Perugino, Pietro
    The Crucifixion and Saints 75, *80*
Petre, Hon. Edward 15
Petre, 11th Baron 13, 15
Philipe, Gérard 103
Phyffers, Theodore 51, *51*
Pignatelli, Fr Joseph 97
Pinter, Harold 109, *109*
Pius IX, Pope 13, 23
Pius XI, Pope 100
Pius XII, Pope 100, 102, 103
Plater, Fr Charles 27
Pollen, Fr John Hungerford 24, *24*
Pollen, Patrick 87, *105*
Poor Servants of the Mother of God 21
Porter, Fr Thomas 65, 66
Portuguese Embassy Chapel, South
    Audley Street, London 14, 15
Powell, James and Sons 43
*Prayers and Devotional Exercises Used at the
    Church of the Immaculate Conception,
    Farm Street, Berkeley Square* 19

Prior Park College, Bath 34
Pugin, A. W. N. 33–4, 37, 51, 60, *107*
    criticism of Scoles 41
    high altar 13, 43–8, *46–7*, 87, 111
    stained glass 43
Punch 11
Purcell, Henry 110
Purdie, Alfred Edward 58, 60, *62–3*, 66, 68,
    68, 70–2, 72, *84*

Quadragesima Anno (1931) 97
'Queen Anne' style 68, *71*

Rattee and Kett, Cambridge 60
Redemptorists 17
Rees-Mogg, William 109
Religious Census (1851) 17–18, *18*
Roberts, Archbishop Thomas 103, 108
Robinson, Fr Dominic 113
Romaine-Walker, W. H. *11*, 43, 68–87,
    72, 74, *76–7*, *84*, *86–7*
Roman Catholic Church
    Catholic Relief Act (1829) 11
    congregations 17–18
    dogma of the Immaculate
        Conception 13
    and establishment of the Church of the
        Immaculate Conception 11–15
    hundredth anniversary of the
        Restoration of the Catholic Hierarchy
        in Great Britain 102
    Religious Census (1851) 17–18, *18*
    revival in England 11–13
    see also Society of Jesus (Jesuits)
Romanos Pontifices 21
Rome 13, 14, 39, *84*, 100
Roper, Fr Harold 60, 103
Royal Academy of Arts, London 48
Royal Opera, Covent Garden 100
Ruddock, Samuel 60
Rudolf, Archduke of Austria and Crown-
    Prince of Austria-Hungary 26, 27
Ruskin, John 51, *51*

Sacram Communionem 107
Sacred Heart Sisters 21
Saffron Hill, London 15
St Barnabas, Pimlico, London 43
St Francis Xavier, Liverpool 37
St George's School, London 112
St Ignatius, Preston 37
St Ignatius College, Stamford Hill,
    London 21
St James, Spanish Place, London 65
St John the Evangelist, Islington,
    London 41
St John's Wood, London 14
St Joseph's Hospice for the Dying,
    Hackney, London 23
St Joseph's Library 94, 102, 108
St Mary of the Angels, Westminster,
    London 20
St Mary's, Horseferry Road, London 15

St Vincent de Paul Society 110
St Winefride, Holywell, Flintshire 34–7
Salviati of Venice 43, 49, 60, 87
Sant'Andrea al Quirinale, Rome 84
Santa Maria Maddalena dei Pazzi,
    Florence 75, 80
Scala Theatre, Charlotte Street,
    London 102–3
Scoles, Fr Ignatius 30, 37, 66
Scoles, John Joseph 33–48, 42, 51, 58,
    72, 91
Scott, Adrian Gilbert 39, 87, 103
Scott, Fr Edward 11
Scott, George Gilbert 37
Second World War 39, 87, 91, 100–1,
    100
Shrewsbury, 16th Earl of 33–4, 39, 48
Sisters of Notre-Dame de Namur 21
Sitwell, Edith 107–8, 108
Society of Jesus (Jesuits) 11
    converts 20, 21–4
    establishment of the Church of the
        Immaculate Conception 11–15
    Manning criticises 20–1, 29
    The Month 23
    Romanos Pontifices 21

Sodality Hall, Farm Street, London 95,
    101, 102
Sodality of the Immaculate Conception
    20, 58, 71, 95, 102
South America 97
The Spectator 108
Das Spiegel 109
'Spy' (Leslie Ward) 29
Steuart, Fr Robert 95–7, 102
Stevenson, Joseph 23–4
Stonyhurst College, Lancashire 13, 20,
    20, 34, 94
Stourton, 18th Baron 13, 15
Street, George Edmund 72
Stuart, Janet Erskine 21
Swynnerton, Joseph
    The Man of Sorrows 76
    Mater Dolorosa 76
Synthetic Society 24

The Tablet 11, 15, 31, 95
Tarrant, Mr 48
Tayler, Albert Chevallier 75
Tayler, James 60
Taylor, Mother Frances (Magdalen)
    21, 21, 23

Tempest, Sir Charles, Bt 13, 33
Tempest, Joseph 43
Tempest, Monica 13, 43
Teresa of Avila, St 23
Thérèse of Lisieux, St 97, 97
Thurston, Fr Herbert 24, 24, 25
Tichborne family 21
The Times 100
Tosca (Puccini) 97
Towneley, Mary Elizabeth 21, 21
Tracy, Fr John 110
Troup, Malcolm 112
Twiddy, Elisabeth 21
Tyrrell, Fr George 24–5, 24, 29

US Embassy, London 101
Usher, Revd P. C. 101

Vatican II (1963–65) 87, 108, 109, 110
Vaughan, Fr Bernard 29, 29, 93–4, 94, 95
Verrocchio, Andrea del 80
Victoria Eugenie, Queen of Spain 27, 93
Viner, Brigadier Gordon 110

Wailes, William 43, 91
Ward, Wilfrid 24

Wareing, William 17
Waterworth, Fr William 19, 19, 24
Waugh, Evelyn 96, 97, 101, 107–8
Weitz, Guy 94, 96, 108
Weld, Fr Alfred 21, 24, 24
West London Day Centre 113
Westminster Abbey, London 72, 112
Westminster Cathedral, London 51, 94,
    107
Westminster Council 103, 112
Whiffen, Charles 72, 75, 75, 76, 80, 82,
    107
White, G. P. 58
Whitty, Fr Robert 20, 20
Wilhelm II, Kaiser 93
Willis & Sons, Henry (organ builders)
    107
Wingfield-Digby, Fr Robert 107
Winkley, Austin 43, 87
Wiseman, Cardinal Nicholas 17, 19, 20, 23
Wispelaere, Alphonse de 74
Woodlock, Fr Francis 97
Woollett, Fr 21
Writers' Library 100, 108

Yujico, Maria Jesusa 110